GREEN GREEN GREEN

GREEN GREEN GREEN

19 Customer-Centric Philosophies to Drive Your Dealerships' Growth

JASON QUENNEVILLE

LIONCREST
PUBLISHING

GREEN GREEN GREEN
19 Customer-Centric Philosophies to Drive Your Dealerships' Growth

FIRST EDITION

ISBN   978-1-5445-4893-7 *Hardcover*
   978-1-5445-4892-0 *Paperback*
   978-1-5445-4891-3 *Ebook*
   978-1-5445-4890-6 *Audiobook*

This book is for my children: Fallon, Seeley; and Brock

CONTENTS

INTRODUCTION

There's nothing quite like the thrill of racing. The roar of the engine, the smell of burning rubber, the sharp turns, and the sheer speed—it's a rush like no other. Racing demands precision, focus, and a relentless drive to be the best. It's about finding that perfect line, making split-second decisions, and feeling the surge of adrenaline as you push the limits of both machine and human. For me, racing has always been more than just a sport. Even though I officially drove in my first sanctioned race at age 40, it's a passion that has been with me since I was a teenager.

I grew up on a dairy farm, where every day was filled with early mornings and endless chores. It was hard work, but it taught me the importance of discipline and perseverance. Amid the daily grind, I found an unexpected source of excitement: racing. I was surrounded by it. I spent weekends watching my uncle, cousin, and mentor—who also happened to be a car dealer—dominate the track that I now race at. Watching them, I always dreamed that one day I'd be out there myself, pushing the limits.

Racing was always in my blood, and as a kid, I did side races and attended racing schools whenever I could. Today, I get to realize my childhood dream: I spend my Saturdays at the track, practicing or competing in dirt modified car racing.

Racing teaches you to trust your instincts, to react quickly, and to stay calm under pressure. It's about teamwork, too, just like running a successful car dealership. Every pit crew member has a role, just as every team member in a dealership plays a critical part. Racing is where I find my clarity and my drive. It reminds me daily of the power of passion and the relentless pursuit of excellence—values I carry with me into every aspect of my life and business.

Racing cars and running a car dealership may seem worlds apart, but the philosophies that drive success in both are remarkably similar. Just as winning on the racetrack demands meticulous preparation, teamwork, and a well-executed strategy, so does achieving success in automotive sales. To be fast on the track, you must ensure the car is perfectly tuned for the specific conditions, whether it's the weather or the unique characteristics of a dirt track. This means relying on a skilled team where everyone knows their role and executes it flawlessly.

In the dealership world, the same principles apply. Every team member must be well trained and understand the entire process from start to finish. Sales, service, parts, BDC, and office—they all need to be in sync, just like the pit crew, to ensure a seamless experience for the customer. If one person isn't prepared or makes a mistake, it can slow down the whole operation, just like a pit stop gone wrong can cost a team the race.

And considering how much customer expectations have changed in recent years (for customers, convenience is now king), alignment, from the sales to the service teams, is even more critical.

In both racing and running a dealership, you need to anticipate challenges and plan for them in advance. Whether it's having a plan for changing tires in a split second or knowing how to handle a customer's concerns efficiently, the key is to think ahead.

Practicing these scenarios, understanding potential obstacles, and refining your processes continuously ensure that you are not just reacting but proactively steering toward success.

By embracing philosophies with these same sensibilities in mind, I have been able to build multiple dealerships that operate with the precision and agility of a top racing team, always prepared, always focused, and always ready to win.

And thankfully so. These philosophies helped all the New Hampshire Toyota dealerships I have managed or owned throughout the years achieve success at multiple levels.

And I'm excited to tell you about each of them.

THE FAILING STORE CHRONICLES

It all started with my first dealership GM position (my *career* started many, many years before that at Chevy, where I worked my way up from Recon, but the philosophies were first implemented in my first dealership GM position).

When I was announced as the GM in 2018, the store was selling only 80 cars a month. When I left in 2020, in my last full month, we sold 286. All thanks to the wonderful team and many of these philosophies.

I was asked to GM a small-town Toyota dealership, also in Vermont (what I'll refer to as Toyota #1 throughout this book), that was in bad shape. The facilities and operations were in pretty decent shape, and the team was (for the most part) stellar, but sales were struggling.

When I started, it was ranked 45th, had a sales efficiency of 103%, and sold 110–120 cars per month. When I left, it was in the top 10, with a sales efficiency of 206%.

And the last month I was there? We sold 286 new and used vehicles.

The secret to my success? I brought the philosophies I had implemented at other dealerships with me. *Together with the incredible team there* (I couldn't have done it without them), we put them into practice and *built* on them—we developed even more automotive philosophies that disrupted the industry for the betterment of both the customer *and* employee.

The second and third Toyota dealerships where I was co-owner and/or GM (Toyota #2 and Toyota #3), both in the Boston Region, had similar stories when I jumped on-board as co-operator: the buildings were falling apart, and operations missed the mark (and were like money pits). In one of the locations, many of the team members were involved in illegal business practices (I discovered the latter after I signed on to help).

Both dealerships had abysmal sales numbers as well, which wasn't surprising. They had bad reputations in the community—no one wanted to buy or service their car at either location.

At the beginning of my tenure as operating partner in 2022, Toyota #2 was ranked 68th in the Boston Region (out of 71), had a sales efficiency of 105%, and was selling 80 vehicles a month.

Today?

It's continuously ranked in the top 15, has a sales efficiency of 157%, and sells more than 200–250 vehicles each month.

Toyota #3 started out in even worse shape: it had a sales efficiency of 84% (way below the franchise requirement of 105%) and was selling 60–80 vehicles per month when I signed up to help in 2019.

As of year end 2024, it had a 300% sales efficiency and sold 200–270 vehicles per month.

At both Toyota #2 and #3, I relied on my philosophies—and the help of incredible teams of automotive sales and service professionals I have the privilege to partner with each day—to change them from failing to *thriving* dealerships where the local community is excited to buy and service their cars and employees are proud to work.

Not convinced? Let me tell you a little bit more.

TOYOTA #3

It was October of 2019.

I had my work cut out for me.

When I stepped in as operating partner, of the 71 Toyota dealerships in the Boston region, it was ranked 64th.

When I first arrived, not everyone was happy to see me. Many employees were comfortable with how things were and were resistant to change, especially following the recent firing of their GM. They were wary of my intentions and skeptical about the changes I planned to implement. Some were openly argumentative (particularly the finance manager), questioning my philosophies and insisting that their existing methods were just fine and didn't need any adjustments.

Despite this initial resistance, the results speak for themselves. Our customer satisfaction ratings have dramatically improved—from a high of 3.9 stars on Google to an impressive 4.9 stars. Customers now love visiting the dealership, often commenting on the positive energy they feel here. The transformation hasn't just been external; our employees now genuinely enjoy their work and are enthusiastic about being part of a dynamic, forward-thinking team.

Within three years, together with an incredible team of automotive sales and service professionals (then and now, I partner with the best in the business), we turned it all around. Today, Toyota #3 is consistently in the top 10 Toyota dealerships in the region and has been as high as 4th.

Pretty incredible, right? The team at Toyota #3 and I are really proud of what we've done. We love what we do and *where* we do it.

Throughout this book, I will showcase *each of* these dealerships to show you how to put the philosophies into practice and, when you do, how effective they can be.

MY AUTOMOTIVE PHILOSOPHIES

Why do these philosophies matter?

If your dealership is failing, they can help you turn it around and *save* it. I know how hard you've worked to build and sustain your dealership because I've been there. With a little help, you can turn it around and protect your legacy *and* your team.

If your dealership is failing, you aren't alone. Before the pandemic, the annual sales rate was 17 million vehicles.[1] In 2024, it reached 15.8 million.[2] Analysts project some growth in 2025, to 16.2 million, but overall, sales are still down.[3]

While new-vehicle inventory levels have improved, leading to more incentives and discounts, high interest rates and tight credit conditions continue to constrain the market, impacting consumer affordability and demand.[4]

We're coming off a COVID-19 high, when supply and demand worked in favor of the dealerships. It was a hot seller's market because vehicle supply was low. Now that supply and demand have evened out, car dealerships aren't hitting their sales numbers because it isn't easy and convenient to buy cars. (After the pandemic, it became easy to buy just about everything else.)

I have been in the automotive industry since 1998. I have worked in every position and have seen just about everything. I have seen what works and what doesn't.

And based on that experience, I have developed 19 tried-and-true automotive dealership philosophies with the sole purpose of improving the customer and employee experiences in order to increase sales.

With the help of incredible teams, I have put these philosophies into practice, and together we have saved multiple failing car dealerships. In each instance, we focused on the customer and employee experiences and built large, loyal customer bases.

All these 19 philosophies can be applied to car dealerships, and *most* of them can be applied to *any* business (even a sandwich shop) because the roots of these philosophies start with empathy and putting on the shoes of customers *and* employees. This approach can guide decisions about pay plans, staffing, and understanding what truly drives customers.

There are many philosophies in this book that, when put into practice, can help save *any* business in *any* industry, not only automotive dealerships.

But regardless of industry, there is a requirement: you have to buy into and really give these philosophies a try. If you half-ass them, they won't work. You can't simply stick your toe in the water—you need to dunk your head in.

RETAIN CUSTOMERS FOR LIFE; SELL MORE CARS

Retaining customers for life, empowering staff, and selling more cars are central to my automotive philosophies.

Green, Green, Green is for *everyone* who wants to turn around their business, but it is mostly geared toward people with pre-existing automotive and car dealership knowledge because it is chock-full of automotive industry terminology that will be challenging for anyone not in the industry. It is for car dealership owners, operators, and executives who want to retain customers, empower employees, and sell more vehicles.

It is also for dealership owners and management staff who are proactive, absorb information, and take decisive actions based on that information. This book is for managers and owners in the automotive industry with decision-making authority who want to sell more vehicles and help their dealership to be ranked higher.

You've probably faced moments when you've looked in the mirror and questioned yourself, wondering, *What am I doing?* It's easy to compare yourself to others or doubt the path you're on. But if you stick it out and commit to seeing things through, the results often speak for themselves. I've learned this firsthand; every time I've persevered and stayed the course, things have worked out in the end.

I wrote this book because I want to share what my teams and I have achieved—I want to help others succeed. When I invite my co-owner and peers to visit our stores, they can see the results of our hard work and the changes we've implemented.

I want you all to see those results in your stores too.

If you want to make meaningful changes at your dealership and need to convince others, this book can be your guide.

These 19 philosophies focus on the customer experience so you can retain your customers no matter the circumstances. I'll show you the approach I've used and how I can personally help you apply it to your situation.

GO ALL IN

It's understandable that some car dealership executives might be hesitant to try these new philosophies and make changes—because the path is harder. To truly cater to everything the consumer wants and make their life easier, the dealership has to take on more responsibilities. That also requires more money, more time, and more energy to sell and deliver each car.

Meeting these consumer expectations means going *all in* to see the benefits. At first, there may be a dip—a kind of J-curve. Initially, it might feel like more work, more expense, and even the need to change staff or incur upfront costs. However, only by fully committing to these changes can you eventually reach the point where the benefits become evident and worthwhile.

It's about having the right mentality—one of diligence and tenacity. This book is for people who possess the resilience to try new approaches, even if they fail, and who have the determination to persevere through challenges. It is also for those who have a genuine love for the automotive industry (like me) and a commitment to ethical practices.

It will not teach you stereotypical car dealership processes or methods; it will teach you the exact opposite. The lessons and philosophies are unorthodox. They aren't for anyone who strongly believes in traditional car dealership sales and service models.

Green, Green, Green is for dealership owners, executives, and general managers who want to try something new to improve the success of their stores. My 19 unorthodox philosophies cover every area of a car dealership, from sales to service and everything in between. They will teach you how to exceed customer expectations at every stage of the customer's car-buying journey so they come back again and again for all their car purchases in the future. They will also show you how to attract, hire, and retain top talent, as your team is central to the customer experience.

SAVE YOUR DEALERSHIP

My team and I sold a lot of vehicles during COVID-19. Almost all dealerships did because it was easy—if the dealership had the cars, customers bought them.

But car buying has changed because the world has changed and our customers' expectations are different. Our customers are now used to instant gratification—they can get just about anything with same-day delivery and have short attention spans.

A study from Northeastern University indicates that the average time a person can focus on a task has decreased significantly over the past two decades, dropping from about 2.5 minutes to around 45 seconds. This decline is largely attributed to the "constant bombardment of information" from digital devices, which makes it harder for people to maintain focus on a single task for an extended period.[5]

They are also well informed. They spend the time researching to find exactly what they want. By the time they reach out to us, the car dealer, they have a very clear understanding of what they're looking for. Often, they know the precise vehicle they're interested in.

If we want to sell more cars, we need to meet customers where they are. We have to come up with new, inventive ways to get them exactly what they want *quickly*.

If we want our stores to be consistently ranked in the top ten...

If we want exceptional sales efficiency (or a similar metric if your dealership doesn't recognize that one)...

If we want to sell hundreds of vehicles, month over month...

We need to put the car-buying experience *first*.

The first thing I do before I race is anticipate challenges and plan for them. I visualize the track and put myself in the shoes of the pit crew and driving team. *What could possibly go wrong, and what is the best way to respond?*

Car racing requires anticipating challenges and working with the pit crew and driving team to prepare for them.

Running a car dealership requires anticipating the needs of the customer and working with the sales and services teams to deliver an exceptional customer experience, one that keeps them coming back.

Throughout my career, I have made it my mission to improve the car-buying experience for my customers no matter the circumstances because I love the automotive industry. It's all I know, and it's all I want to know. I am passionate about my stores and am committed to their continued success.

My philosophies are unusual, but they work. I have improved the sales at multiple dealerships, pre- and post-pandemic, because I focus on the customer's experience. My goal is to put their needs first, always, and thanks in large part to my team, the dealerships I run consistently overperform and have some of the best numbers in the region.

I want dealership owners and GMs like you to have the best numbers in *your* region too. I want to help you sell more cars because I want to see you and your dealership succeed.

If you have a store that you *know* can perform higher...

If you *know* you have a dealership with the capability to sell more cars...

I am confident my philosophies can help.

CHAPTER 1

CHALLENGES IN THE AUTOMOTIVE INDUSTRY

In 2019, on the week of my 40th birthday, I bought into Toyota #3.

I knew the store wasn't doing well—it was ranked 64th (out of 71 dealerships in the Boston Metro Region), was way below the required sales efficiency percentage (84%), and was selling 60–80 vehicles a month—but I decided to buy into the store anyway. I had turned around a few dealerships before, Toyota included, and I was confident I could do it again.

I had banked my life savings on it.

But when I walked into the store the second day after purchasing it, I quickly became sick to my stomach.

I was setting up my office in what could only be described as a makeshift closet. The place was old and rundown, with 1950s wood paneling, no air conditioning, and even bullet holes in the glass. As if that wasn't bad enough, I heard a noise above my head.

Suddenly, a ceiling tile fell, and a river rat dropped right out of the ceiling and skittered across the floor.

It was a stark contrast to my previous store, which was beautiful, situated at the intersection of two interstates with a newer building that was spotless. The difference created a lot of anxiety and stress. Now, instead of a prime location, I was stuck in a rundown building 20 minutes down a winding back road, filled with rats and surrounded by grumpy people.

I had a mortgage on my house and had spent a year and a half putting money into this dealership. I left a very secure position with deferred compensation and walked away from a hefty paycheck to come here. The decision made me physically sick.

Plus, everything about the way Toyota #3 was run went against my methods and best practices, automotive philosophies I had honed since starting in the industry in 1998. I knew what the sales numbers were when I bought in. What I didn't know was *how* the dealership operated to get those numbers.

With a few exceptions, the staff operated in stark contrast to the principles I believed in. The team had been trained to focus on setting appointments without providing any pricing information, operating under the belief that the best way to secure a sale was to get customers into the dealership first and convince them to buy.

I had turned around underperforming stores before, but this one was in really bad shape. I went home on my birthday in tears. When I got there, I threw up, convinced I had screwed everything up. I felt utterly defeated while I stared at the wall, questioning everything.

What made matters worse was that one week later, I received a letter from Toyota North America threatening to shut Toyota #3 down.

ACTION PLAN REQUESTED

From: TMS

Sent: Tuesday, October 22, 2019, 11:47 AM

To: Jason Quenneville

Subject: Action Plan Request

Hi again Jason,

Please provide/submit an action plan with your dealer application to improve sales efficiency at Toyota #3. The dealer is sales deficient at 87.6% through Aug 2019 on a rolling 12-month basis versus the minimum requirement of 90%.

Thank you and LMK if you have any questions.

TMS

Market Representation Analyst

Toyota Motor North America

I stared at the letter. I knew how bad the store was performing before I bought into it. And I knew it was even worse than I thought the second I stepped inside.

But I wasn't expecting to receive the letter. I was shocked.

I had spent my entire life savings to buy 25% of Toyota #3. If the store was shut down, I would lose everything.

Unless it could be saved. My teams and I had done it several times before, so why not now? I had been in the industry for decades and had turned around many underperforming Toyota dealerships in the region. We had improved the sales numbers for those stores using 19 unorthodox automotive philosophies I had curated since 1998, when I first started working in the industry.

My team and I had done it before, and we could do it again.

From: Jason Quenneville

Sent: Monday, October 28, 2019, 8:03 AM

To: TMS

Subject: Re: Action Plan Request

TMS,

As I have just taken over this store on the 1st of October and have not been a part of the deficiency up to this point, I will be changing everything. I will start with the culture and staff, making sure to surround myself with forward-thinking people who have empathy and a hospitality background. Second, we will be heavily focused on our digital marketing and change how we handle our incoming leads. Third, the inventory was handled by a salesperson prior to my arrival. I have taken this over and will be stocking correct inventory and managing a 45-day turnaround. Fourth, I have exited all third-party warranty providers and banks. I will be using my relationship with Toyota Financial and only their products to help sell more Toyota vehicles and provide a higher service retention rate. Fifth, I will teach my consultants how to handle every part of the sale from lead to F&I. This will give our customers a better experience, help grow my staff, and empower them to be more efficient with less turnover. These actions are just a sample of the changes we will be making. Going forward, we will be sales efficient, and there will be no need for another action plan!

Sincerely,

Jason Quenneville

Within two years of using those philosophies, my team and I increased the underperforming dealership Toyota North America had threatened to close to a 303% sales efficiency. Toyota #3 became the most sales-efficient store in the region.

COLLECTIVE SUCCESS

Turning the store around required a comprehensive strategy that started with how we handled leads and marketed for new ones. We had to rethink how our inventory was displayed to attract more customers, which meant changing our marketing approach to bring people in. I knew that once we got the leads, we needed to handle them differently to convert them into sales.

I faced serious resistance at first. Two people quit because they didn't agree with the new methods for handling leads, and another openly argued with me, claiming that giving customers too much information would allow them to shop around. It felt like a constant battle: my philosophy against their reluctance to change. I knew I had to stay firm. Having the right support was crucial; without it, it would have taken much longer to turn things around (more on how critical the right people are in Chapter 7, How to Hire).

And it did. In the first month, we sold 134 cars, up from the 60–80 Toyota #3 was averaging before October 2019, proving that the new strategies were effective. From there, we implemented a disciplined approach with daily training sessions, constantly preaching the philosophy and explaining why these changes were necessary. Even when some of the staff didn't fully believe in the new direction, those who did stayed the course with me. As *everyone* started selling more cars and making more money, they *all* became believers.

Getting the staff to buy into the new system was critical; that meant showing them positive returns quickly—within the first month—otherwise, I risked losing their support.

By demonstrating the benefits early on, I fostered a team that believed in the vision and was committed to collective success.

UNDERSTANDING CONSUMER EXPECTATIONS

In today's digital age, consumer behavior has shifted dramatically. People are accustomed to the convenience and efficiency of online shopping platforms, where they can browse, compare, and purchase products with a few clicks. Reviews, speed of delivery, product details, cost transparency, and little to no human interaction have become standard expectations.

The automotive industry doesn't work like that. Today's consumers seamlessly interact with a computer and a delivery person for most purchases, but at a car dealership, they are expected to call for pricing, interact with multiple people across multiple touchpoints, and spend half a day there in person.

Can you see the disconnect between what customers expect today and how most car dealerships currently do business?

Retailers across industries are leveraging technology and innovation to enhance the customer experience and retain customers. Technological innovations such as artificial intelligence (AI), augmented reality (AR), and self-service options are becoming standard tools for enhancing customer satisfaction and driving customer retention. AI is being used to personalize shopping experiences by analyzing customer data to predict preferences and tailor marketing efforts, thereby improving customer engagement and loyalty. Retailers are also adopting AR to blend online and offline shopping experiences, allowing customers to virtually try on products or visualize items in their own space before making a purchase. These technologies not only meet the evolving expectations of tech-savvy consumers but also provide a more interactive and engaging shopping experience.[6]

The faster car dealerships can provide customers with information and streamline the purchasing process, the more likely they are to earn the customers' business. Studies show that consumers are willing to pay more for a superior customer experience—according to research by SuperOffice, 86% of buyers are willing to pay extra for it.[7]

Yet many dealerships have been slow to adapt. While other industries rapidly embrace customer-centric strategies to differentiate themselves and retain customers, some dealerships still rely on traditional models that do not prioritize customer experience. This hesitation to adapt can lead to missed opportunities for increasing customer loyalty.[8]

ACCELERATING CHANGE

COVID forced businesses to adapt. Nearly 72% of retail professionals reported that the pandemic accelerated their company's digital transformation by at least a year.[9] Door-to-door delivery became the norm for everything from groceries to electronics. Consumers became used to convenience and personalized experiences. Now they expect the same in all their transactions, especially when making a major purchase, like buying a new car.

During the pandemic, automotive sales were fantastic. The

demand was high, and the supply was low, so dealerships could charge whatever they wanted (for the most part).

The reason behind the high demand for new cars but a shortage in supply boils down to a perfect storm of supply chain issues, particularly a global shortage of semiconductor chips. These tiny chips are a crucial part of modern cars, controlling everything from entertainment systems to advanced safety features. When the COVID-19 pandemic hit, it forced chip factories around the world to shut down, halting production. Without these chips, car manufacturers simply couldn't build the vehicles they needed to keep up with demand.

The demand hasn't changed, but supply is back up, consumers' expectations have changed, and the industry hasn't adjusted its sales processes or customer experiences.

NAVIGATING INDUSTRY SHIFTS

Dealerships are struggling to get into the rhythm of sales after COVID-19. That's because consumer expectations have changed.

How do you think the car-buying experience compares to experiences offered by online shopping and food delivery companies?

For most, a vehicle is the second-most expensive purchase they will make. It should be a smooth, efficient, and *enjoyable* process. Car buyers should have a great experience when at a dealership so they come back for their second, third, fourth and fifth car.

If the car-buying experience is exceptional, your customers won't go anywhere else ever.

But focusing on the customer experience is a big change for most dealerships—owners, GMs, and sales executives have been trained to focus on the numbers. Convincing these automotive industry leaders to embrace change and adapt to changing consumer expectations is tough. Despite success stories from other dealerships, many remain resistant to abandoning traditional practices. Transitioning from a focus on sales to one on the customer experience is significant and requires buy-in from all staff at all levels. Changing practices requires a fundamental shift in mindset. How can we expect our sales and service personnel to put the customer's needs first if the executives don't believe it's important?

The customer experience is critical, and it starts with your employees on the ground floor, but expectations have changed for our employees too.

In an era when work-life balance and culture are important, dealerships must prioritize employee satisfaction and well-being. They also must work hard to attract top talent. You can have the nicest service tech in the world, but if they don't know what they're doing, the customer will leave feeling dissatisfied. Their experience will be piss-poor. Offering competitive benefits, fostering a positive work environment, and adapting to changing employee expectations are necessary today to attract top talent.

And isn't that what we all want: to attract the best so we can enhance the customer experience and sell more cars?

THE NEED FOR CHANGE

In today's landscape, the customer experience should be priority number one, and we have online shopping and delivery service companies to thank. These companies' customer-centric approaches set a new standard for consumer convenience and efficiency. The circumstances of the world have adjusted what our employees expect too.

When I received the letter from Toyota North America threatening to shut down Toyota #3, I was terrified. I thought I was going to lose everything.

But I dug my heels in, put the customer experience first, and focused on training staff and attracting top talent. Within a year, using the tool kit of philosophies I curated over decades of experience, we went from one of the lowest-performing Toyota dealerships in the region to one of the highest.

Through dedication, perseverance, and a commitment to customer satisfaction, we transformed the struggling dealership into a thriving enterprise. Since 2020, Toyota #3 has consistently seen a sales efficiency rating of over 300%, been in the top 10 of dealerships in the region, and sold 200–250 cars, new and used, month over month.

CHAPTER 2

HOW THE AUTOMOTIVE INDUSTRY CURRENTLY DOES BUSINESS

My family shops online a *lot*. We buy essentials like paper towels and toilet paper and receive a couple of boxes almost every other day. Online shopping has become our go-to for everything from clothing to cleaning supplies and even coffee. It's more affordable.

It's also more convenient. Besides the cost savings, we prefer online shopping over going to physical stores because we don't have time to shop. The convenience of doorstep delivery, coupled with its vast selection and user reviews, make it incredibly easy to shop and compare.

And this convenience factor isn't exclusive to online shopping. It extends to food delivery services too. One of the dealerships

I bought into is within five minutes of a McDonald's, but the staff often orders delivery. To save them the hassle of leaving the building, they are willing to pay *three times more* to have their food delivered right to the office.

It all comes down to the value of time versus money. Today, most people have more money than they do time.

YOUR CUSTOMER'S CAR-BUYING JOURNEY

I want to ask you to take a moment to put yourself in the shoes of your customers during their car-buying journey. Let's look at the experience from their perspective.

Kathy has been thinking about buying a new car for months. She has done her research and knows exactly what she wants. She looked up your dealership online and found the exact make and model of the car she's looking for in your inventory.

So she heads to your dealership to get more information.

As soon as Kathy walks in, she's back at square one. She's greeted by a salesperson who sits her down and asks her questions about what she's looking for, even though she's already self-identified those things. The goal of the interview? To steer Kathy toward a purchase that aligns with the dealership's agenda rather than her preferences.

So Kathy sits at the dealership for hours, despite her prior preparation.

If she goes through with the purchase, her experience doesn't end there—she will need to talk to a sales manager and a finance manager who will try to upsell additional products, even after she's settled on a specific payment plan. This additional layer of negotiation can feel burdensome, adding complexity to what should be a straightforward transaction.

And when she's ready to drive off the lot, she'll interact with someone completely different to review the car with her before finally concluding the transaction.

Now, compare that buying experience to the buying experience with online shopping.

Which do you think your customers prefer?

SALES AND THE SHOWROOM

The goal of almost every car salesperson is to get customers into the showroom. When customers reach out to the dealership, whether by phone or online, traditional sales methods push to bring them in. They want their customers mesmerized by the vehicle they're test driving. They believe that once infatuated, the customer will no longer be concerned about payments.

Suppose that customer inquires about a trade-in value over the phone. Instead of providing a straightforward estimate, the salesperson they're speaking to will likely insist on inspecting the car in person, citing factors like mileage and condition. Before the customer knows it, they have an appointment to come in and have their trade-in inspected.

Even if the customer expresses an interest in knowing the best price before coming to the dealership with their trade-in, the salesperson will continue to steer the conversation toward an in-person visit.

"Quoting a price without experiencing the car firsthand risks losing your interest."

Traditional car salespeople are very good at sidestepping direct inquiries. They make it impossible for customers to get answers without first stepping into their showroom.

IT STARTS WITH MARKETING

Traditional dealerships thrive on this elusive approach. They don't give away pricing details, trade-in values, or payment options until the customer is physically present.

And it all starts with marketing.

Picture this: a dealership has a fleet of twenty RAV4s. To get customers interested, it selects the most budget-friendly model available and creates a tempting offer with hefty down payments and every conceivable rebate under the sun, from college student to military discounts.

When a potential customer calls in to ask about the advertised deal, they're met with enthusiasm and assured that the car is still available. But when they get to the dealership, the advertised car has conveniently been sold.

The dealer has a similar option available, but it's more expensive—it isn't eligible for rebates and is subject to additional fees, including taxes and hidden charges.

The aim of this bait-and-switch tactic? To hook customers with incredible offers and get them in the showroom.

Dealerships often invest heavily in marketing, spending anywhere from $10,000 to $150,000 a month on various strategies, ranging from digital campaigns to traditional methods like radio and print ads. However, tracking the return on investment (ROI) for these efforts can be incredibly challenging. The data provided by marketing companies can sometimes be manipulated to show more favorable results, making it difficult to know which strategies are truly effective.

For example, radio advertising might be useful for announcing a big promotion or event, but it's nearly impossible to determine if a radio ad is responsible for a specific sale. You can't always tell how a customer heard about your store, and that makes it tough to gauge whether the money spent on radio ads is actually paying off.

This issue isn't limited to radio; even grassroots marketing efforts, like local sponsorships or community events, lack clear metrics for measuring effectiveness. As a result, marketing remains one of the biggest expenses for a dealership, yet there is often no straightforward way to assess its impact.

It's crucial to focus on the customer experience. When customers have a great experience, they're likely to tell everyone they know, providing valuable word-of-mouth marketing that doesn't cost a thing. On the other hand, a bad experience can lead to even more people hearing about it, which can harm the dealership's reputation. While I still believe that spending money on marketing is important, I've found that you don't need to invest as heavily in it if you ensure your customers leave happy and satisfied. A positive customer experience is, in many ways, the most effective and cost-efficient marketing strategy of all.

WHAT ABOUT THE SERVICE DEPARTMENT?

I've noticed a trend toward focusing on customer experience in the service departments of most dealerships. Many are making strides to emphasize a more customer-centric approach by implementing technologies like e-payments and video multipoint inspections (MPI). With e-payments, transactions are faster and more convenient, while video MPI allows a customer to see real-time footage of their vehicle's condition, fostering transparency and trust. Additionally, advanced systems now recognize customers as soon as they arrive, enabling a more personalized service experience.

There's also a push to revamp business development centers (BDCs) in service departments to manage not just scheduling but also customer communications across digital channels, making interactions more seamless and efficient. These innovations are all about enhancing customer satisfaction and building loyalty.

But there are still many dealerships that do not have these advantages, which leads to unnecessary upselling tactics.

Take the process of scheduling a service appointment, for instance. A customer makes the call, sets up an appointment, and heads to the dealership, only to find themself bombarded with unnecessary upsells. It's a frustrating experience that often leaves the customer feeling misled and dissatisfied.

In a traditional service department, when a customer calls to schedule an appointment for their 20,000-mile SUV service, the typical process is straightforward: set the appointment, and have the customer bring the car in; then get the vehicle on the lift for inspection. However, issues often arise when the technician finds additional problems, like worn brakes or a dirty cabin air filter. Suddenly, the customer, who expected a simple service with a set price and time, is now told it will cost significantly more—perhaps $1,000 extra—and require several more hours to complete. This unexpected news disrupts their day and adds to their frustration, as they're forced to spend more money and time than planned.

My approach is different. When a customer calls to schedule their 20,000-mile service, my team and I take extra steps to pull up all the relevant information about their car. We check for any recalls, review the service history, and assess the condition of components like the brakes. If we notice the brakes were at 5 mm during the last visit, we anticipate they might need replacement soon. We discuss this with the customer over the phone, explaining the possibility of additional time and costs, and provide an estimated price upfront. Unlike traditional dealerships, we believe in being fully transparent, even quoting prices over the phone to help customers make informed decisions.

This way, when the customer arrives, they're already aware of what to expect regarding both time and cost. Many are more willing to drop off their car, knowing there won't be any surprise charges unless something unexpected happens, like a new issue discovered during the inspection. This method also allows us to manage shop capacity more effectively. Instead of underbooking with the hope of upselling, we plan our schedule to accommodate around 70 appointments a day using 13 service bays, ensuring everything runs smoothly without inconveniencing customers. While upsells are sometimes necessary, they are reserved for genuinely unforeseen issues. By asking the right questions upfront—whether the car still has its original brakes or when it was last serviced—we set the customer up for a much better experience that builds trust and satisfaction.

A car-buying experience at one of my stores is a whole lot like online shopping.

HOW ONLINE SHOPPING WORKS

Operations for online shopping companies go a little something like this.

They have warehouses where they store products from various vendors. They then market them and sell those products.

They utilize in-house staff who communicate via Zoom.

The primary objective is to maximize sales. The company does that by providing a wide range of options and making the selling process as convenient and straightforward as possible.

Online shopping makes the shopping experience convenient, streamlined, private, and personalized for the customers.

Online shopping is highly transparent because customers have access to photos, reviews, and upfront, fixed pricing—what you see is what you get. This level of clarity reduces uncertainty, as customers know exactly what they're buying and can easily return products if they're unsatisfied. The no-risk nature of online shopping has set a standard for transparency that other industries, including car dealerships, are now being pushed to match.

ONLINE SHOPPING IS CONVENIENT

Online shopping is convenient. It is also cost-effective—it costs less in time than shopping in person. For my family, time is our most precious commodity.

Most people today are willing to pay more for convenience, something car dealerships can leverage to their benefit. Imagine this: you hand-deliver your customers their brand-new cars, albeit at higher prices than the dealership down the road. But here's the catch—the dealership down the road requires its customers to spend four or five hours of their valuable time at the dealership, and you *don't*. You bring the car directly to the customer, handle all the paperwork electronically, and ensure a seamless experience.

For today's customers, there is a price point where convenience becomes invaluable.

Online shopping companies get that. Their entire business model was built around it.

ONLINE SHOPPING IS STREAMLINED

Online shopping is all about convenience, offering a streamlined process where customers can click, add items to their cart, check out, and be done. Research is made easy on the company's website, with all the necessary information provided upfront, ensuring a hassle-free checkout with nothing hidden. In contrast, dealership websites often encourage customers to contact them, aiming to bring customers into the store for the sale. Online retailers provide all details upfront, aligning with my approach—those who come in are already prepared to make a purchase.

Currently, when individuals step into most dealerships, they are met with a fragmented process that lacks personal connection. They interact with a lot of different people—a receptionist, a salesperson, a finance manager, and a check-out attendant. When customers shop online, they only interact with themselves. Today's customers don't want to interact with more people than they have to; that's why shopping online is so great.

ONLINE SHOPPING IS PRIVATE

I had a client recently who wanted to purchase a car as discreetly as possible. She valued her privacy and wasn't comfortable sharing personal information in a public setting like a dealership. She was concerned about the amount of sensitive information she'd have to provide, such as her income, Social Security number, credit history, and mortgage details. Understandably, she didn't want to discuss these matters openly where others might overhear.

To accommodate her, we decided to handle everything online. She appreciated dealing with just one person who could manage the entire process from start to finish. This way, she only had to provide her private information once, directly to me, ensuring it stayed confidential. The online environment made her feel more secure, much like when buying something expensive online, where privacy and discretion are paramount.

We also took extra measures to ensure the security of her transactions, just as we do when securing credit card information for online purchases. This gave her peace of mind, knowing that her personal data was protected. She was able to complete her purchase without ever stepping foot in the dealership, feeling reassured that her privacy was maintained throughout the entire process.

By providing this level of security and discretion, we were

able to meet her needs perfectly, demonstrating that even in car sales, we can provide the same level of privacy and comfort as any high-end online purchase.

Privacy is another factor. Sometimes people don't want to broadcast what they're buying; some people prefer the privacy of online shopping. An online purchase delivered directly to their doorstep is discreet.

ONLINE SHOPPING IS PERSONALIZED

Online shopping is discreet and private. It's also personalized.

I think we're all well aware of online shopping companies' use of AI for tracking—it's integral to their business model.

In this regard, the auto industry isn't too far behind. Toyota and other OEMs are leveraging AI to monitor search histories. For instance, if you browse baby strollers online, expect to see ads for Sienna vans pop up in your social media feed.

Many OEMs are chatbots (more AI tech), to enhance the customer experience by making it more seamless and efficient. These chatbots collect customer information and quickly direct customers to the specific service or information they need, reducing human interaction. This automated approach not only simplifies the customer's buying and service experience but also allows OEMs to track customer behavior more accurately, providing personalized service and improving overall satisfaction.

Many customers are thrilled with the personalized experience AI offers in online shopping, especially when compared to the shopping experience they get in traditional stores, which is shaking up our industry.

People receive convenient, streamlined, private, and personalized shopping experiences *every single day* because they are shopping online and ordering takeout.

This is all the more reason it's critical to not only understand today's customer's expectations but to *exceed* them.

PRIORITIZE TRANSPARENCY AND EMPOWER CUSTOMERS

The way people prefer to shop and spend money has changed. They are used to convenient, streamlined shopping experiences that are private and personalized. They have these shopping experiences every single day, and they get them for the little things, like groceries, toiletries, and McDonald's.

So what do you think they expect their shopping experience to be like for *bigger* purchases, like sporting equipment, luxury goods, and vehicles?

For most people, their car is the second-most expensive thing they'll buy, so the auto industry needs to offer a comparable or *superior* experience to the ones customers get online shopping.

Hyundai is doing it. It has partnered with Amazon to revolutionize the car-buying experience. Soon, customers will have the option to buy a car entirely online.

Some dealerships might be skeptical, believing that customers still crave a personal touch. While this might be true for some, many customers are dissatisfied with the current dealership experience and are willing to sacrifice personal interaction to avoid feeling pressured or uncomfortable.

Today's customers expect a different shopping experience, and they're willing to pay for it. They want convenience. They want to interact with as few people as possible. They want what they're buying to be private (in many cases), and they want it *all* personalized.

This week, five online shopping packages have been delivered to my house, and twelve of the employees at one of my stores have ordered McDonald's online.

And it's only Tuesday.

Traditional dealerships don't offer this type of shopping experience. Most thrive on an elusive, in-personal approach. They shy away from divulging pricing details, trade-in values, or payment options until a customer is physically present, which is very inconvenient and not at all private. They then inundate that customer with half a dozen in-person interactions.

It's enough to make any modern-day customer's head spin.

The traditional dealership experience can be convoluted and time-consuming, with multiple layers of interaction that don't always align with the customer's best interests. This fragmented approach often leaves buyers feeling overwhelmed and underserved.

But my teams and I do the exact opposite. Instead of playing into these outdated tactics, we challenge the status quo. By prioritizing transparency and empowering customers with upfront information, we break free from the confines of traditional dealership norms.

My philosophies are a departure from the conventional automotive dealership playbook, but they resonate with today's customers who want honesty, transparency, and integrity (and convenience, privacy, and personalization) in their car-buying experience. They also speak to dealership employees who value the same.

Now that we are aligned with how the car dealership industry currently does business, it's time to disrupt it using my 19 automotive philosophies.

CHAPTER 3

19 AUTOMOTIVE PHILOSOPHIES

I love to cook because I genuinely enjoy eating good food, and there's something incredibly satisfying about preparing a meal that tastes amazing. I work out 4 days a week, not just for fitness but so I can indulge in delicious meals guilt-free. There's a special kind of pleasure that comes from crafting a dish to perfection and then watching others enjoy it as much as I do. Seeing people savor every bite of something I've prepared makes all the effort worthwhile, and it's this shared experience that makes cooking and grilling so rewarding for me.

I love to cook, and I especially love to grill.

When my old grill broke recently, I decided it was time to upgrade, and I wanted to invest in something truly special. My research and the reviews I read painted a clear picture of the strengths of the brand I decided to purchase. First and foremost, the quality stood out—customers frequently praised the products for being durable and long-lasting, which is exactly what I look for in a grill. The brand's website also impressed me; it was easy to use and navigate, and it provided all the information I needed to make an informed decision. The imagery was so good that it felt almost tangible, like I could touch the grill right through my screen. This attention to detail and focus on providing a seamless online experience reinforced my decision to choose a great grill from a great company.

Excitedly, I placed my order and eagerly awaited its arrival, and true to their word, the company reached out to me on the day of delivery, offering to guide me through the assembly process via Zoom.

I felt confident in my abilities and opted to follow the emailed instructions and video tutorials they provided instead, but the offer was meaningful because it showed that they were willing to take the time to ensure I was completely satisfied with their product. They didn't have to go to such lengths, but they chose to go above and beyond to make sure I was happy.

This kind of customer service is rare and demonstrates their commitment to not just making a sale but building a relationship with their customer. It was this willingness to go the extra mile that made their offer stand out and feel genuinely valuable to me.

The grill surpassed my expectations in both performance and craftsmanship, but what truly set this company apart was its unwavering commitment to customer satisfaction.

They proved their commitment to customer satisfaction right from the start when I initially purchased the grill. The company offered to help set it up, which made the entire process much easier for me and showed that they genuinely cared about my experience. The purchase itself was straightforward, with no hidden steps or complications, which added to the overall positive customer experience. From beginning to end, everything was handled smoothly and efficiently, reinforcing that the company's focus was on making sure I was happy with my decision and satisfied with their product.

From the initial purchase to ongoing support, they went above and beyond to ensure my experience was nothing short of exceptional.

A DEDICATION TO SERVICE

I continue to receive thoughtful follow-ups and updates from the grill company. Their dedication to service has earned my loyalty; I respect their brand and will buy their grills for life.

Many car dealerships are like this retailer; they understand how important it is to exceed customer expectations and earn lifetime loyalty.

But many are not. These dealerships focus on maximizing profit margins in the short term and, in the process, ignore the customer's needs. Today's customers expect instant gratification and door-to-door service.

Do you think they'll go back to a car dealer that didn't meet their expectations?

Successful car dealerships today must *exceed* customer expectations to cultivate lifelong customer relationships.

That's why my philosophies work. They exceed expectations because they focus on customer-centricity and transparency. These philosophies prioritize customer satisfaction and cultivate lifelong customer loyalty, which drive profitability.

Car buying should be a joyful and exciting experience for customers and an enjoyable one for employees.

My philosophies enhance the employee experience by creating a work environment that is easy, honest, and transparent. Employees don't have to hide anything or feel pressured to act unethically; instead, they can be open and straightforward with customers. This honesty allows them to feel good when they go home at night, knowing they made someone's day better and were genuinely helpful.

Car buying should be fun, not just a transaction focused on how much money we can make. When employees are proud of their work and feel valued, they are happier, and happier employees naturally sell more cars. By fostering a culture that prioritizes customer satisfaction and transparency, we create a positive atmosphere that benefits both our staff and our customers.

My philosophies are built on a foundation of enhancing customer loyalty, simplifying decision-making processes, and prioritizing the customer experience.

And I've been developing them throughout my career.

BE PROACTIVE AND ADAPT

At 17 years old, I got my start washing cars at a local Chevrolet dealership as part of a recon team for a brief 4-week stint. At 44, I co-own two dealerships (Toyota and Mazda) in New Hampshire.

I got to where I am today because I have challenged the norm and pushed the limits of the car dealership status quo, all for the sake of the customer experience.

It started with one pivotal moment: the decision to eliminate interest rate markups. I was a sales manager at the time and was up to date on the latest automotive industry news. President Obama was in office, and it seemed as though interest rate regulations via the Consumer Financial Protection Bureau (CFPB, a US government agency) were inevitable. I wanted to be proactive and adapt, so I got approval from the store owner to develop my first automotive philosophy (in this book, it's Philosophy 11)—I removed those markups and was upfront and transparent about pricing and payments.

By doing that, my team and I created a culture of trust and empowerment for everyone.

And sales increased.

We increased sales *and* redefined what it means to buy a car in today's market; we prioritized transparency, empathy, and customer satisfaction.

Our marketing costs decreased too. Most car dealerships typically spend $50,000–$150,000 on marketing each month via radio ads, internet ads, billboards, and mailers. And most of their efforts can't be tracked. They don't know if the customer on the phone or in the showroom hears about the store on the radio or reads about it in a mailer.

We spend about $20,000–$25,000 per month on marketing because most of our customers are either referrals or repeat customers.

This is thanks to my philosophies.

These philosophies are designed to be outside the box, moving away from the approach of a traditional car dealership. They focus on what both customers and employees truly want and expect from their experience. By emphasizing the importance of both groups, we recognize that you can't have one without the other; a happy employee leads to a happy customer and vice versa. These philosophies put both the customer and the employee first, ensuring that every interaction is positive and rewarding. This not only enhances the overall experience for everyone involved but also fosters a more collaborative and supportive environment within the dealership.

As the automotive industry continues to evolve, my philosophies serve as a foundation for those seeking to create a more customer-focused approach to automotive sales and service that also increases the dealership's bottom line.

CUSTOMER EXPERIENCE CORE IDEAS

Starting when I was a sales manager, I gradually implemented my philosophies, which gained me the autonomy and the authority to reshape dealership practices. My philosophies increase sales, all while centered around creating a better, more ethical environment for both customers and employees.

These 19 philosophies have transformed dealerships into thriving businesses. They guide my approach and shape the experiences our customers have when purchasing their cars and the experiences my team has when selling and servicing those cars.

The employee and customer experiences are all that matters. With that in mind, these philosophies focus on the customer experience and center around these core ideas.

1. MAKE DECISIONS EASY

Customers should find it easy to make decisions because time is valuable. When it's hard, people won't do it. If your website is disorganized, for example, they will think *you* are disorganized.

Make the decision-making process easier for your customers by empowering your teams to have all the necessary information at their fingertips. This requires extensive training to ensure that employees are well versed in pricing, vehicle details, payment options, and available incentives.

By making this information readily accessible—whether through the dealership's website or in person—customers can quickly find what they need without feeling overwhelmed or pressured. When customers feel informed and confident, the decision-making process becomes much smoother and more enjoyable, ultimately leading to a better overall experience.

Be respectful of how much time you're spending with your customers. Whether it's choosing a car or navigating through the buying process, simplicity is key.

Studies show that a frictionless or hassle-free customer experience significantly impacts customer satisfaction, loyalty, and purchasing behavior. For example, customers who have a seamless, easy interaction with a company are more likely to complete purchases and become repeat buyers. Research indicates that a smooth customer journey can increase conversion rates and drive revenue growth. Companies that prioritize a frictionless experience see a 1.6-times increase in customer lifetime value and a 1.4-times boost in revenue compared to those that do not.[10]

When customers find the experience hassle-free, they're more likely to make a purchase.

2. PRIORITIZE CUSTOMER ACQUISITION

Instead of focusing solely on maximizing profit from each individual customer, my philosophies aim to attract as many customers as possible. At each of my stores, my teams and I do so by creating a sense of fun at the office.

We have fun at my dealerships on "Jersey Fridays"—they have had a noticeable impact on the atmosphere.

(I got the idea for Jersey Fridays from a friend who owns and operates a dealership in Florida—I'll tell you the origin story at the beginning of Chapter 5.)

When an employee has worked at one of my dealerships for one year, they receive a "team" jersey. When they hit service milestones—5, 10, 15, 20 years, etc.—they receive a patch to affix to their jersey. On Fridays, everyone wears their jersey. It's a lot of fun.

Customers often notice when the staff participates, and it adds an approachable element to their visit. I remember one time at Toyota #2 when a customer was so intrigued by the group of us in our jerseys that they took a photo (for us) and wanted to know what was happening. Their excitement was contagious, and it created a unique connection that could even inspire future employees. This lighthearted tradition helps create a welcoming environment where people feel comfortable and enjoy doing business. By fostering a positive and friendly atmosphere, we make the dealership a place both customers and employees want to be.

Jersey Fridays create a sense of fun and foster ease in the car-buying process. In turn, that increases sales.

3. EXCEED CUSTOMER EXPECTATIONS

I firmly believe that exceeding customer expectations is what sets successful car dealerships (and all businesses, really) apart.

At Toyota #1, I remember a customer we had in New Jersey who couldn't drive up to pick up their car. So one of my team members drove the car down to New Jersey, personally dropped it off with the customer, and took the train back home. The customer was in awe and beyond grateful for the experience.

By putting the customer first, ensuring transparency, and providing helpful assistance before, during, and after the purchase, we create loyal customers who *enjoy* buying cars.

4. BE TRANSPARENT AND ACCESSIBLE

Transparency and accessibility are nonnegotiable in our approach. We provide easy-to-understand information about products and pricing—we give our customers all the information upfront. They can visit the dealership's website or call in to receive the latest up-to-date information about vehicles we have on the lot. We give them accurate pricing and payment details.

We also simplify the payment process and organize the website for seamless navigation. We ensure that customers have all the necessary information at their fingertips so they can make their car-buying decisions *before* they come to the dealership.

5. MEET CUSTOMERS WHERE THEY ARE

When customers shop for cars online, they invest a significant amount of time—on average, about 18 hours—researching before making a decision. During this time, they're carefully considering everything from the vehicle's make and model to color, interior features, and payment options. In today's market, the worst thing we can do is make a customer repeat that entire process when they finally walk into the dealership. That's why meeting the customer where they are in their buying journey is key.

The Toyota brand offers a digital tool, SmartPath, that allows us to seamlessly pick up right where the customer left off (more on this later in the book). Whether they're in the middle of purchasing a RAV4 or exploring leasing options for a Camry, these tools provide us with insights into exactly what stage of the process they're in. Instead of sitting customers down and asking them questions solely for our benefit, we use this data to continue the conversation, focusing on what matters most to them.

By doing this, we eliminate redundancies and frustrations. Our team can jump right into the specifics, addressing any final details the customer may have missed and guiding them smoothly to the finish line. This approach not only saves time but also builds trust, as the customer feels understood and supported throughout their buying experience.

Understanding the customer's car-buying journey is crucial. Whether it's through an online shopping experience or a personalized consultation, we meet customers at their preferred touchpoints, including payment, vehicle display, and location. No matter what it is, we try to meet customers where they are and ensure their experience is tailored to their needs.

6. FOCUS ON THE LONG-TERM APPROACH

The long-term approach in a dealership isn't only considered after a sale is made; it's an ongoing strategy that begins well before the first transaction and continues far beyond it. The key is to provide a great experience from the very start, ensuring that customers feel valued and satisfied. When customers have a positive experience, they are more likely to return for future needs, providing a second opportunity for the dealership to engage with them. The goal is not just to make a single sale but to cultivate a relationship that encourages customers to return, potentially bringing their entire family along as well. It's not about maximizing the profit from each individual transaction but rather focusing on the volume of sales over time.

Traditional automotive dealership metrics often prioritize immediate profits. My approach is long term. Prioritizing customer satisfaction and loyalty creates a sustainable business model that benefits both customers and the dealership in the long run.

I believe in building long-term relationships with customers by offering exceptional service before, during, and *after* the sale. This generates repeat business and fosters positive word-of-mouth referrals, ultimately contributing to the overall success of the dealership.

These core ideas speak for themselves. Our stores consistently ranked among the highest in the region for internet closing ratios, a testament to the effectiveness of prioritizing customer experience over profit margins. And by nurturing long-term relationships, focusing on the customer experience, and delivering exceptional service, we saw an increase in service volume, positive word of mouth, and overall business growth.

TRANSFORM THE WAY YOU SELL CARS

Customers today expect hassle-free shopping, door-to-door service, and easy returns.

For all their purchases.

My favorite grill retailer gets this. The customer's experience is their top priority at *all* points during the journey.

And that's not all.

During a massive storm, wind whipped my brand-new grill off my two-story deck and dropped it on the ground.

I was devastated. I had only used it once.

But the grill company came to the rescue. They hopped on the phone with me and instructed me on how to fix it. They didn't have to do that—I had purchased the grill weeks earlier. Their commitment to me and my experience with their grill has made me a customer for life.

It is clear this company's approach is to put the customer first.

I believe in this approach for car dealerships because I've seen it work. By prioritizing the customer experience above all else, I've witnessed increased sales and service volume firsthand. Positive word-of-mouth marketing, generated by satisfied customers, further enhances business and reduces the need for traditional marketing efforts.

By providing holistic solutions that meet the customers' needs and expectations, my team and I embrace transparency, deliver the experience customers desire, and focus on long-term relationships rather than short-term gains. That's why it's critical to meet customers where they are and sell them cars on their terms, whether that's delivering cars to their doorstep or providing a seamless online buying experience.

These philosophies have been the cornerstone of our dealerships' success in the industry. They have helped us sell more cars and make more money because they serve as a roadmap for transforming the way car dealerships sell and service cars; they also create an enjoyable experience for both customers and employees. By prioritizing transparency, simplicity, and customer satisfaction, we pave the way for a future where buying a car is no longer a dreaded chore but a delightful experience.

And with companies like my favorite grill retailer leading the way, I'm confident that we're on the brink of a paradigm shift that will redefine automotive retailing for generations to come.

Now, without further ado: Philosophy 1.

CHAPTER 4

ORGANIZATION AND FLOW OF BUSINESS

Philosophy 1

As the door swung open, I entered the lobby of Toyota #3 with anxious anticipation. From the lack of organization in the parking lot (I had no idea where to park when I first pulled up), I knew I was going to have my work cut out for me to turn the store around.

But what greeted me was far from what I expected—what I saw was pure chaos. Personal belongings were scattered everywhere haphazardly. Inventory keys were in a pile on the floor, and desks were cluttered with paperwork. There was very little room for actual work to get done.

The physical state of the store only added to the chaos. The building dated back to the 1950s, and it hadn't been remodeled or even maintained. Bullet holes were etched into the glass. Weeds were growing out of the building and the old panel walls. Inside, there was no AC, and it smelled like mold. Paint was chipping off the walls, and ceiling tiles were missing. The building was gross.

The place reeked of mildew and disorganization...for the employees and the customer. There were no signs to guide customers, so they wandered aimlessly, unsure of where to go or who to approach for assistance. And the attire of the staff added to the confusion—there were jeans, T-shirts, polo shirts, and the occasional suit and tie. So it was difficult to discern who worked there and who didn't. It was easy to see customers' frustration as they struggled to navigate the disorderly store.

I was also frustrated because senior leadership was absent. With no clear direction or support from above, everyone seemed to be vying for control, and employees were left to fend for themselves amid the showroom chaos.

The service department mirrored that chaos. Service cars were intermingled with retail vehicles, creating a logistical nightmare. The service manager, in the absence of senior leadership, attempted to assert control over every aspect of the operation. This led to a toxic work environment. The manager's behavior, characterized by bullying and yelling, created low morale among the team. Employees were visibly stressed and unhappy, and the atmosphere was tense and unproductive.

Despite the overwhelming chaos, I had hope. Toyota #3 needed a lot of work, but the first step was simple and easily achievable: the dealership itself needed improved organization and flow.

ORGANIZATION VS. FLOW

The organization and flow of your business are your top priorities because of two reasons:

1. They impact the business's entry point and the first thing customers and employees see.
2. They help maximize business efficiency, which minimizes the amount of time a customer spends inside a dealership.

We've established that for many of our customers, time is their most valuable currency. Consumers increasingly demand instant, easy access to products and services—instead of driving up the street to pick up a fast-food hamburger, they have it delivered via an online app. They don't care if they have to pay more for the convenience; they place a higher value on their time.

Companies that fail to meet these expectations, including car dealerships, may struggle to remain competitive. Central to meeting these new expectations are the organization and flow of your business—how it looks (where products and sales desks are placed) and operates (who handles what and how long the sales process takes).

Organization is the strategic arrangement of resources to achieve a specific goal. In the context of a business, it encompasses cleanliness, discipline, and professionalism. A well-organized environment fosters efficiency and adds to a positive company culture. It also influences customer and employee perceptions and shapes their experiences and interactions with the brand.

Flow, on the other hand, refers to the smooth and continuous movement of people, information, and resources throughout the organization. It creates speed by minimizing bottlenecks and reducing the likelihood of mistakes. Time is precious, so flow is crucial in optimizing processes and maximizing productivity. Flow ensures employees and customers can easily navigate the space. It creates a sense of comfort and convenience.

In a dealership environment, customers expect to find products readily accessible (and sales staff readily available to assist them). Inefficient organization and flow can lead to frustration and confusion, jeopardizing the customer experience and ultimately impacting sales. By centralizing departments, such as sales and finance, and implementing communication protocols, such as text messaging (more on all that in upcoming chapters), businesses can maintain professionalism while improving the customer experience.

The ease of navigating a physical store is important for customers but also for employees. By prioritizing organization and flow, businesses can create environments that are conducive to success, in terms of both customer satisfaction and employee productivity. Investing in these aspects of business operations is critical in today's fast-paced and competitive landscape.

THE IMPACT OF PERCEPTION

Organization and flow impact the overall perception of the dealership. They're the customers' first impression of the business.

The *digital* flow of business is included in this too. For website-visiting customers, how your website looks and its navigational ease matter.

When I step into a New England home valued at $4 million or more, I expect to be met with opulence and grandeur. If I see a decrepit building invested with vermin instead, I will be very confused. Shocked, even.

Now, consider a $4 million *business*. I expect sophistication and professionalism when I walk in the door, so if I encountered an environment that feels more like a rundown, failing business, I would turn right back around.

First impressions matter for customers and employees. Assessing and improving the flow of business—from appearance to operations—can significantly impact their experiences.

Recognizing the importance of perception and its impact on customer and employee morale, the leadership team and I prioritized restoring order at Toyota #3. We also organized the parking lot and interior layout.

We marked parking areas clearly and designated walking paths so everyone knew precisely where to park and how to get to where they needed to go when they first arrived. We also reorganized the lot to create a more welcoming and orderly appearance. I personally took on the task of cleaning up the grounds, even going as far as mowing the lawn myself when I arrived—it was nearly a foot long! These efforts made a noticeable difference in the dealership's curb appeal, helping to create a more professional and inviting environment for customers as soon as they drove onto the lot.

For the building's interior, we invested in paint, cleaning supplies, and bleach, and we meticulously cleaned up every inch of it. This included decluttering and reorganizing the space.

In a traditional dealership setup, various departments are typically scattered across different locations within the facility, leading to inefficiencies and communication challenges. Sales offices, finance offices, and paperwork processing areas are often segregated, making it difficult for employees to access information quickly and seamlessly. Customers are often shuttled between different offices, causing delays in the sales process and overall frustration. This disjointed approach can lead to a game of ping-pong, with information bouncing back and forth between departments.

So one of the first things we did was remove all the sales desks from the showroom floor and relocate all the salespeople to an old conference room we cleared out on the building's second floor. This change allowed salespeople to move freely around the showroom, making them more readily available to assist customers without being confined to specific desks.

At the same time, this setup kept the managers close to their teams, ensuring they were accessible whenever the sales staff needed support or guidance. The removal of fixed desks reduced physical barriers, promoting a more collaborative and responsive atmosphere where managers could easily transition between helping customers and assisting their teams.

This also reduced the need for customers to navigate multiple locations for their transactions.

The combination ultimately improved their experience and increased our customer ratings.

The changes also helped improve office culture and employee morale—people were working together to sell cars *and* keep the space clean.

In the service department, changes were implemented to enhance customer comfort and convenience. This included setting up a waiting room with amenities like a TV, flowers, AC, carpet, new chairs, and fresh paint to create a welcoming atmosphere. We also installed clear signage to guide customers on where to drop off their vehicles for service, facilitating a smoother intake process.

The importance of cultivating a positive workplace culture was also recognized. This involved fostering a collaborative atmosphere among staff members. We did that by organizing training sessions and setting a dress code, which promoted professionalism and teamwork. From the appearance of the lot to the professionalism of the staff, all aspects of the business exuded an air of excellence.

Sales processes changed too. Reorganizing where the sales team did their work made it much easier for them to access critical information quickly. This restructuring also involved placing management and staff in the same central area, which facilitated better communication and collaboration.

As a result, answers were provided and responses were given

much faster, streamlining the overall sales process and improving efficiency throughout the dealership.

When I walked into Toyota #3, I was shocked by what I saw. The goal was to create an impression of a multimillion-dollar business and leave all visitors (from all walks of life) impressed and satisfied. I had turned around underperforming, disorganized stores before, but I had my work cut out for me.

Bottom line: with the help of an incredible team, we implemented Philosophy 1: Organization and Flow of Business and sold and serviced more cars, increased employee retention, and made more money.

But organization and flow are only as good as your dealership's culture and communication, which we'll talk about next.

CHAPTER 5

CULTURE AND COMMUNICATION

Philosophy 2

Remember Jersey Fridays? I want to tell you the story about how Jersey Fridays got its start here in New Hampshire.

Throughout the years, I've made a ton of incredible industry friends. A few of those friends own dealerships.

One day, while I was visiting a good friend's dealership in Florida, I noticed that almost all his employees were wearing matching jerseys with the dealership's name and logo.

"What's all this?" I asked.

"It's Jersey Friday," he explained. "After employees have been here a year, they get a jersey. Every Friday, we all wear our jerseys."

I loved the idea so much, I asked if I could steal it.

"Not only am I OK with that, but I promote it. Jersey Friday is one of the best things I did for my store."

When I got back to New Hampshire, we started Jersey Fridays right away at all my dealerships. I communicated the concept at the team trainings the next day and bought jerseys for everyone in the store who had been with the dealership for longer than a year.

Then, the leadership teams and I took it a step further.

We decided that on the first Friday of every month, we would recognize birthdays *and* work anniversaries. In addition to giving out jerseys to employees on their first anniversary with the dealership, we would give out jersey patches for every year of service.

We also chose to give out monthly awards for the top salesperson, top service tech, employee with the best attitude, and employee who best demonstrated the dealership's core values. These employees each received a handwritten thank-you card from me and a gift card.

We also celebrate our employees' service anniversaries with a fun Wheel of Fortune game. Starting with their first year, team members spin a colorful wheel marked with dollar amounts ranging from $10 to $100. The amount they land on is multiplied by their years of service—for example, five years at $50 equals $250. It's a lively way to recognize and reward employee dedication.

To celebrate our President's Award (a monthly award given to an employee who exemplifies key values), we host a memory competition. The winner studies a pattern of letters, symbols, and shapes and then recalls as many as they can. The number they remember becomes a prize multiplier, with a maximum of 10.

These traditions highlight our team's achievements while adding a little fun to the workplace.

They're one of the reasons the culture at my dealerships is so strong and attractive (and employee retention is so high). We reward loyalty and make it *fun*.

CULTURE IS PEOPLE

Company culture is critical to the success of your dealership, something many traditional dealerships overlook.

Not focusing on culture results in a money-driven, cutthroat dealership that gives customers a bad feeling the minute they walk into the store. They can tell when they're talking to someone who only cares about how much money they'll make. When the culture inside a dealership is financially driven, customers can feel it.

Ultimately, culture revolves around people—their attitudes, interactions, and experiences. We want a dealership culture so strong, so positive, it's contagious. We want customers to walk into our dealership and think, *It feels* good *in here. I want to buy a car.*

In the long run, ignoring culture will likely result in fewer sales because if employees are unhappy or don't get along with their coworkers, it creates a toxic environment that can lead to lower productivity and poor customer interactions. In a sales environment, this is particularly damaging because sales rely heavily on building rapport and trust with customers. When the culture is poor, employees are less likely to go the extra mile to engage with customers, which can result in fewer sales.

A poor culture doesn't just affect sales employees; it can impact every level of the dealership, from management to service staff. If people are not working well together, it creates friction that disrupts the entire workflow. Just as in industries like construction or dairy farming, where teamwork and a positive work environment are crucial for daily operations, the same applies to a sales environment. When employees are not in sync, productivity drops, morale plummets, and, ultimately, sales decline.

On the flip side, a positive culture directly impacts employee motivation, productivity, and customer interactions. When employees are happy at their jobs, they are more engaged and motivated, which means they don't constantly watch the clock, and they actually look forward to coming to work. This positive energy is contagious and can significantly enhance the customer experience, making customers feel more welcomed and valued.

By fostering a positive culture where employees feel valued, connected, and motivated, dealerships can create an environment that supports higher sales, better customer service, and overall success. Ignoring culture not only risks the immediate dissatisfaction of employees but also threatens the long-term viability and profitability of the dealership.

HOW WE DO CULTURE

Customers today want an enjoyable experience. That starts with the dealership's culture.

Culture is one of our priorities. Our objective is to cultivate an environment where employees and customers feel genuinely positive, so we focus on the following:

- Team building
- Human resources
- Training
- How to hire (which includes recruiting and competitive compensation and benefits)

Training and How to Hire are so significant, they have their own dedicated philosophies (3 and 4, respectively). We'll cover them in the upcoming chapters. For now, let's focus on team building and human resources.

TEAM BUILDING

What is team building?

Team building is about fostering collaboration and cooperation among employees to achieve stronger, more effective results. When people work together, their combined efforts lead to better outcomes than if they worked individually. Team building can occur both internally and externally, with activities designed to help coworkers get to know each other better and create stronger bonds. These stronger relationships enhance the overall workplace culture, making the environment more enjoyable and productive for everyone. By encouraging employees to build trust and camaraderie, team building contributes to a more cohesive, supportive, and motivated workforce.

Many dealerships do team-building events with their employees. We do a lot of them throughout the year, in addition to Jersey Fridays, because we believe employee morale is important for selling cars. A study by the University of Oxford's Saïd Business School found that happy employees are 13% more productive. These employees work faster, make more sales, and use their time more effectively compared to their unhappy counterparts. Additionally, happy employees are more likely to engage positively with customers, enhancing customer satisfaction and loyalty, which can lead to increased sales and better overall business performance.[11]

Every quarter, the leadership teams and I throw a BBQ and potluck at each dealership. I grill up a variety of meat, and employees bring the sides and desserts. We also host Race Track Day, where we all drive go-karts around an indoor track.

Race Track Day is one of my favorites (I love to floor it in a go-kart and leave the team in the dust), but our quarterly engagement dinners are a favorite too. A nice meal is catered after hours, and everyone is invited. The cost of entry? They have to come up with one idea that benefits the customer or employee experience.

And they have to be willing to stand up and share their idea with everyone.

There is always someone taking minutes during the engagement dinners. After the meeting, all the ideas are put into a slide deck for management to review. We select our favorite idea, and the employee who came up with it gets to work with the management team on developing and implementing it.

Here's a good employee idea we implemented: we installed a bell that rings whenever a customer buys a car. This creates a celebratory atmosphere in the dealership. It's a simple yet effective way to acknowledge each sale and make the moment special for both the customer and the team.

It also gives everyone the right to stop what they're doing to congratulate the customer as they leave the store. This adds a personal touch and makes the customer feel appreciated. These practices not only boost team morale but also enhance the customer experience by making their purchase memorable.

HUMAN RESOURCES

Human resources (HR) is essential for maintaining fairness and equality across a company, ensuring that all employees are treated the same. HR's role includes protecting the dealership by managing consistent raises and promotions, ensuring fair treatment, and creating clear job descriptions for all positions. They conduct one-on-one meetings and annual reviews and handle corrective actions to hold employees accountable. HR also facilitates tough conversations and uses tools like anonymous surveys to gather feedback, helping identify employee strengths and areas for improvement to enhance overall workplace culture and performance.

Following HR protocols and best practices is critical to running a successful dealership because they can help with implementing strategies like performance improvement plans (PIPs) when employees are underperforming.

PIPs can be quite helpful because many times employees aren't aware when their performance is subpar. With the right support, they can potentially evolve into top performers.

It's also important to acknowledge and celebrate employees' successes, and HR plays a crucial role in this by helping to create a positive and motivating work environment. When an employee performs well or makes noticeable improvements, HR can implement reward systems to recognize these achievements with bonuses, public recognition, or other incentives. Celebrating these successes helps boost morale and encourages continued effort and growth.

HR also tracks and highlights key performance metrics, such as service profitability and customer reviews, ensuring that these achievements are noted and celebrated. This recognition should not only be limited to the highest-performing individuals but should also focus on those showing significant improvement or growth. This approach promotes a culture of continuous development and encourages all employees to strive for excellence.

Additionally, HR can facilitate exercises to help management better understand their team's performance and recognize contributions. For example, HR might organize an exercise where sales managers review performance data—like average sales units, positive customer reviews, and profitability—without knowing which employee the data belongs to. By analyzing this data, management can identify patterns and see that their assumptions about top performers might be incorrect. This realization encourages managers to pay closer attention to all employees and acknowledge both large and small wins.

Reinforcing positive behaviors helps foster a culture of recognition and appreciation.

HR, the management team, and I also believe in promoting from within, and one of our key priorities is training and grooming future leaders within the company.

So we sent out employee surveys to identify their primary drivers. The top of the list? Financial rewards, lifestyle considerations, and opportunities for career progression. In particular, succession planning.

We understand the importance of investing in our employees and providing them with the tools, resources, and opportunities to advance in their careers. Our training and development programs align with these drivers (more on that in the next chapter) because we want to attract and retain top talent and create a culture of continuous growth and advancement within our dealership.

This is a strategic approach, so our leadership pipeline remains strong. There have been some instances of external hires, but the majority of our management team has risen through the ranks. It's evident by the 4-year service patches they have sewn into their dealership jerseys.

PROACTIVE COMMUNICATION

A dealership's culture is only as strong as its communication, both externally and internally. When everyone in the store communicates effectively, magic happens. The customer experience enhances, and sales and service orders increase. And ratings and stats improve.

When communication is subpar, culture breaks down, and things fall apart.

Traditional dealerships often miss the mark and fail to communicate effectively. They aren't proactive with their approach—they are *re*active. For example, I have heard many stories of traditional dealerships failing to inform their employees about changes until after the changes have already been implemented.

Employees are typically told, without explanation, "This is the change. Do it."

But most people resist change when they don't understand the reasons behind it. And if they feel comfortable with the current system and believe their job performance is good, implementing a new system without clear communication can lead to resentment. This lack of understanding could cause employees to undermine the change or even contribute to its failure.

Many changes come from high-level management who may not fully understand the day-to-day realities of the employees' work. If decisions are made based on assumptions or secondhand information, employees might view management as out of touch or even authoritarian. To avoid this, it's crucial to explain the impacts of any changes on their roles and involve them in the process. A collaborative approach means that changes are more likely to be accepted and helps everyone be more successful.

Involving employees in the decision-making process not only helps them feel valued but also taps into their unique insights, which might highlight considerations that management over-looked. The people who perform the job daily are often best positioned to suggest practical improvements.

When a completely different system is introduced without employee input, it's likely to be met with resistance or resented. I experienced this firsthand when my partner made significant changes to our dealer management system (DMS) without consulting me. As a 25% owner, I believed I should have been involved in the discussion. If I had been, I may have been able to assess the changes *before* they were implemented. I may have been able to save us all a lot of time and money.

THE IMPACT OF A FLAWED SYSTEM AND FORCED CHANGES

The DMS was changed to cut costs, but it ultimately cost us more because it delivered subpar results and a flawed system we struggled with for a long time.

A flawed system of any kind can have a significant impact on a dealership, affecting nearly every aspect of its operations. Because the systems act as the heartbeat of the dealership, any major change or flaw in these systems can disrupt the entire workflow.

Implementing a change or dealing with a flawed system impacts everyone in the store across all departments. It can alter the daily routines of employees, from printing repair orders and processing bills of sale to generating financial statements and ordering parts. Such disruptions can lead to confusion, inefficiency, and frustration among staff, ultimately impacting customer service and satisfaction. When every department is affected by a flawed system, the overall effectiveness and smooth operation of the dealership are compromised, leading to potential losses in both revenue and customer trust.

Forced changes, especially ones with significant consequences, can be detrimental. In this instance, the change over the longer term cost us more money than it saved because it was slower and clunkier, and it resulted in fewer sales.

ACTIVELY INVOLVE STAFF

The change to the DMS wasn't communicated to me, which caused financial loss and frustration. But navigating that challenge made me recognize the importance of considering the human impact of change—it showed me how I should approach change in my dealerships moving forward.

The change isn't only about me; it's also about the people who depend on selling cars to earn a living.

So management and I actively involve the staff in the process.

Effective team communication involves actively involving *everyone*; it's counterproductive to implement changes without team input. We like to encourage open dialogue about the pros and cons of each choice, and after we discuss the options together, we reassure the team that we'll follow up once decisions are made. When we do, we also show them how these changes will improve both the customer and employee experiences.

We don't always get 100% buy-in. But by considering the insights we do receive, together with management, we can make more informed decisions and avoid unnecessary disruptions. Involving employees in discussions also helps gather valuable data and perspectives that may not have been considered otherwise. Even if the final decision goes in a different direction, acknowledging their input makes employees feel respected and understood, fostering a positive and collaborative environment. This approach ultimately leads to a quicker, more efficient result, as the people doing the job are more aligned with the goals and processes of the organization.

What's more important is that everyone understands the rationale behind the changes and feels valued for their input.

EVERYONE LOVES JERSEY FRIDAYS

Jersey Fridays are a hit. Both for the employees and the customers.

Just last week, one customer in particular was so taken by the jerseys that she offered to take a picture of the team wearing them.

And not too long after that, she bought a car.

Everyone loves Jersey Fridays, customers *and* employees. There is a different energy in the dealerships those days—employees are a little happier and more joyous. There's more laughter.

It's fun to be at the store those days. And on the *first* Friday of the month, when we acknowledge anniversaries and birthdays and hand out awards, some employees come in to participate, even when they aren't on the schedule.

We prioritize team building and employee communication (including getting their buy-in on changes) *every* day. Employees like working here, and customers like to shop here.

And everyone knows a good reputation really matters.

So does training. It's important to make sure everyone on the team is aligned. That philosophy is coming up next.

CHAPTER 6

TRAININGS AND MEETINGS

Philosophy 3

Within my first week at Toyota #1, I knew changes needed to happen quickly, starting with how we approached trainings and meetings. I gathered the team together for our first meeting on a Saturday morning and laid out my vision.

"Starting Monday, we're coming in at 8:00 a.m. for training," I said, emphasizing that this was going to be our new routine. For those on the morning shift, we'd start with an 8:00 a.m. meeting; for the afternoon shift, we'd meet at 12:30 p.m. These sessions were dedicated to improving communication and refining our processes. This wasn't just a one-time thing—this was going to be our new normal.

I could tell from the team's response that they were interested and curious. The vibe in the room wasn't resistance; it was more like a collective willingness to see where this new direction could take us. People showed up because they wanted to see what was next, and it set the tone for how we'd approach growth from that point forward. It was a pivotal moment, one that solidified our commitment to daily improvement.

Trainings and meetings are cornerstones of my car dealership practice. Ever since Toyota #1, my teams and I have implemented consistent, daily trainings, morning and afternoon, at every car dealership I have managed.

WHY TRAININGS AND MEETINGS?

When I started with Toyota #1, as you can imagine, there were no trainings or meetings. There were no consistent, non-factory-required training sessions at all. And meetings? I was pretty sure the conference room hadn't been used (for the purpose of meetings anyway) in years.

Trainings and meetings are important because they help ensure performance and customer interaction are the same across-the-board, shift to shift. They communicate changes to processes and protocols consistently, so everyone at the dealership is on the same page. They also help explain the why, which makes it more likely the employees will buy in to the change.

Every dealership is required by the factory to train and certify its staff regularly. Quarterly product trainings, ad hoc sales trainings, and reactive trainings when someone makes a mistake are all required. There are annual OEM certifications, too, and these training courses are usually taken online.

But what about onsite, in-person trainings for dealership-specific best practices?

And what about meetings?

Most dealerships don't have daily, onsite trainings or meetings where they invite collaboration from the junior members of the team. So performance, from sales to the service team and everyone in between, is inconsistent, and decisions are made in a silo and without the input of the employees.

Trainings and meetings are important because the help with the following:

- Communication
- Discipline
- Respect
- Momentum
- Fun

At my dealerships, trainings and meetings are held daily.

COMMUNICATION

We already talked about how important communication is to the success of your dealership today. Trainings and meetings support good communication, internally and externally because they get everyone on the same page. When the trainings and meetings are consistent, the impact is consistent. This helps improve the experience for your customers and your employees.

If there is going to be a change to how the dealership does business or its best practices, we host a training. For example, leasing is coming back to the store—we haven't done any leasing for three years. We need to host a training on the benefits of a lease, how to calculate a lease (by hand), and how to handwrite a lease—and how to communicate all that to the customer.

DISCIPLINE

I believe in daily onsite trainings and meetings, so I worked with my team to schedule two, one in the morning and one in the afternoon, to cover the dealership's two shifts. These trainings are a requirement.

Requiring the staff to show up at the same time daily to train creates discipline. This helps in maintaining consistency and ensures that everyone is on the same page with the dealership's processes and procedures.

The trainer, who covers both, is learning discipline too. A month in advance, they are given their training date and topic. It is up to them to plan and practice their sessions. Everyone in the dealership has the opportunity to lead a training session, even technicians, and the trainers typically rotate weekly. People who don't like to train still get something out of it. It's good for the whole staff.

RESPECT

Daily trainings also establish camaraderie and respect for one another. At each of my dealerships, we are all growing together. We are learning from each other's mistakes and challenges and celebrating one another's victories and wins. We watch videos and critique client interactions. Seeing our fellow employees mess up, and then learn from it, creates deep bonds and mutual respect.

Here's a quick exercise you can do with your team to build camaraderie and respect:

- Everyone stands in a circle; one person is holding a tennis ball.
- That person throws the ball to someone, and a topic is determined.
  - One example is: "Tell me something personal about yourself."
- Every round is a different subject, but they must avoid topics such as sex, religion, and politics.

- We like to start with personal questions to break the ice, followed by general questions about work experience and style and, finally, specific career growth questions.
- If someone feels uncomfortable answering the question, they can simply pass the ball to another person.

Below is a list of 10 different things you can ask while throwing the ball:

- What's something you're passionate about outside of work?
- Do you have any pets? Tell us about them.
- What's your favorite hobby or activity to do in your free time?
- Can you share a memorable travel experience you've had?
- What's a book or movie you recently enjoyed and would recommend?
- What is your favorite movie and why?
- Do you have any unique skills or talents that people might not know about?
- What's a goal you're currently working toward, either personally or professionally?
- Can you describe a challenging situation you've overcome and what you learned from it?
- Who is someone you look up to and why?
- What's one thing on your bucket list that you hope to accomplish someday?
- Why do you work here?
- What skills do you recommend someone concentrate on to focus on sales?
- Why did you get your master diagnostic certificate so soon?
- What is the significance of trainings like this?

This exercise gets people moving and thinking. All the while, I'm listening and learning, from questions they ask, what drives them, how they think, and the respect they have for the company and one another.

Employees who respect one another benefit the dealership by fostering a positive work environment and enhancing teamwork.

FUN

We're also having a lot of fun. Our trainings are fun and engaging, and rarely boring, and we've been doing them for so long now that they've gotten really good. There was a Jeopardy-themed training session that was designed to compete with the other stores I co-own and manage—the trainers kept score. It was educational and fun.

When someone doesn't host a good training session, we all hear about it. And no one wants to be shown up, so people typically put a lot of effort into it and prepare for weeks.

There is no-stop laughter at these trainings. It makes work more fun, and employees who enjoy their work environment are more engaged and motivated.

MOMENTUM

My trainings are daily—at the very start of each shift. When the training is done, employees immediately get started with their workday.

In traditional dealerships settings, employees mill about when they first get to the dealership. They chat up fellow employees, grab coffee, and check their email before they do anything productive.

When the day *starts* with a training session, there's no time to do any of that. Employees have the momentum to immediately get started with their day.

MY EMPLOYEES ARE ALIGNED

One Saturday, I personally hosted a daily training at Toyota #1. I started by counting all the people in the room. There were 10. I wrote 1 through 10 down on 10 little pieces of paper and threw all the numbers in a hat.

I then asked everyone in the room to draw one. When numbers were drawn, I explained the following numbers would work together: 1–3, 4–6, 7–10. The assignment? They were to break off and, within 10 minutes, find something they all had common ground on. After that, their job was to sell the rest of the room on that thing and get us involved.

I also asked each of the three groups to choose one person to present. I then disqualified that presenter to keep the rest of the team on their toes.

I am very competitive, so I turned this into a competition. I told them management would judge, and the team with the best presentation would win a little bit of money.

That added a little fuel to the fire, and I watched as each team presented with the hope of winning the prize. It was fun, motivating, and engaging.

Our sales rankings consistently blow everyone away because all my people know what they're doing. The reviews for the store are glowing because my employees are aligned.

We've come a long way from that first training and meeting, but the results are undeniable. As soon as the staff saw an increase in sales and an overall improvement to the store, trainings and meetings became something they genuinely looked forward to.

Trainings and meetings are critical for employees you already have on staff.

What about the staff you need to hire?

CHAPTER 7

HOW TO HIRE

Philosophy 4

I met Tully in 2015 when he was 20; I was the GM of Toyota #1, and he needed a job.

His life and work history made him an excellent candidate for one of my stores. He had been in foster care for a couple of years as a young kid, and he had leveraged that experience to get a job (through a nonprofit) working with troubled kids—he helped them learn how to cope, taught them life skills, and helped with their school work as their trainer, teacher, or tutor.

He then began working in the nonprofit sector, managing court-ordered programs for various large organizations with multiple locations. He was often assigned to work one on one with more developmentally challenged children, helping them learn basic skills and ensuring they didn't hurt themselves or others.

Afterward, he transitioned to being a personal trainer, a role he pursued for a while with aspirations of opening his own gym. He decided to join a car dealership to gain business experience and learn how to run a successful enterprise, and though it started as a means to an end, he found a place in the industry.

A FAST STUDY

When he started working for me, it was clear he was very loyal and hardworking. He was always a very serious and dedicated employee who came to work with a clear purpose. From the beginning, he was well liked and easy to get along with, but what set him apart was his commitment to taking his career seriously—something that is rare in new employees.

He was also a fast study. He quickly learned my philosophies on selling cars because it was how he would want to buy them. Throughout his training, and even to this day, Tully always thinks about the needs of the customer (and employees) first. He isn't afraid to push back. "If I were a customer, I wouldn't want that."

Tully played a big part in changing and improving our internet lead process, helping us to refine our approach and make significant progress. His contributions helped us enhance our processes and achieve better results.

PARTNER WITH HR

When hiring, it's important to look beyond just finding a buddy, friend, or someone you'd like to hang out with. Instead, focus on finding someone who shares your vision and whose way of thinking aligns with yours. You want to hire someone whose mindset and approach to work are in sync with your own. It's not about forming friendships outside of work; it's about finding someone who naturally understands and resonates with your philosophies because they are common sense to them as well. The key is to hire individuals who have the same sense and sensibilities as you, ensuring a strong alignment in values and work ethic.

Before I tell you how to find candidates like Tully, employees who are loyal, empathetic, and customer centric, I need to stress the importance of partnering with HR for all your hiring.

Hiring is so important that the management team and I partner with the head of HR from the very beginning. We work with them to create a job description, and we try to sit in on every interview we can (the interviews I can't sit in on, Tully takes my place). This way, the employee already knows either Tully or me when they start working for the store.

Most traditional dealerships don't have an HR department. This is a problem because it leads to recruiting and hiring inconsistency. It can also lead to bad decisions overall. HR is there to help dealerships make *good* hiring decisions. I can't tell you how many applicants we've turned down because they didn't pass HR's background check.

RECRUITING 101

HR helped me find Tully, which is why working with them on how and who the management team and I hire has been critical to the success of our dealerships. Tully was an incredible hire—he has undoubtedly contributed to the success of every store he has touched.

But just like a good hire can help your business grow, a bad hire can make sure it shrinks. Your recruiting efforts need to be strong so you can avoid these bad hires.

Here's a quick breakdown of how we recruit for our stores:

1. VET

Once the head of HR and the hiring manager have approved the job description, the job gets posted, and the recruiting process begins. Typically, HR reviews résumés and conducts phone interviews to screen candidates before inviting them to meet with the team in person. This is the stage where we screen for character traits like empathy and a good work ethic.

Traits to Look For

We hired Tully because he's empathetic; we knew it would be easy for him to learn and practice my automotive philosophies. My philosophies are customer and employee centric; they are not fixated on the bottom line. Tully was an excellent candidate for my dealership because he understands empathy.

When we hire salespeople for my dealerships, we don't hire from within the automotive industry. We have found that those individuals tend to be stuck in their traditional automotive ways. It's difficult for them to get on board with my unorthodox philosophies. Instead, we hire people who have empathy and other character traits centered around customer satisfaction, like honesty and integrity.

We love to hire people from the hospitality and service industries because they are customer satisfaction experts. Hotel and restaurant staff at all levels are typically empathetic and customer centric—they prioritize the needs of the customer. We have had such good luck with the hospitality and service industry folks I've hired that I carry business cards with me wherever I go so I can recruit people with exceptional customer service skills whenever I encounter them.

Good work ethic and positive energy are character traits we look for too. These are characteristics of athletes, who we also like to hire. We typically determine whether someone has competed in sports at a high level during the interview process. If we hear someone was the captain of their sports team (even in high school), we become very interested. This quality is indicative of someone who can grow and be a team player and who has high energy. We aren't looking for the goon on the hockey team who spent most of their ice time in the penalty box—we're looking for the captain of the basketball team, the leader of the pack.

2. INTERVIEW

Interviewing is an art in and of itself. First and foremost, we always conduct our interviews with others. Usually, the future manager, future fellow employees, and I are all in the meeting together. Everyone prepares for the interview ahead of time and is willing to answer all the candidate's questions.

Questions to Ask

Knowing the right questions to ask during the interview is often what gets dealership owners, operators, and general managers the most mixed up. Here is a list of questions we typically ask during our interviews:

- Can you take me back to your first career job and briefly tell me about it?
- What did you do day to day?
- Did you get any promotions?
- Did you get any demotions?
- Why did you leave?
- Can you take me through your first career job to today?

Did you notice that we use the word "briefly" when asking candidates to describe their work history? This is intentional to see how brief they can be.

We ask them a lot of questions in a row to gauge their listening skills. Are they able to remember all the questions in the right order? If not, how many do they miss?

We're also gauging honesty. If they skip over a question and when we call them out on it, they hem and haw, we know they'll likely do that as an employee.

Here's another round of questions for you:

- If your advisors and teachers were to describe you in a paragraph they thought you were never going to read, how would they describe you?
- What would their constructive feedback be?
- If we had to let you go 60 days from now, why would that be?

The answers to these questions tell me what the candidate needs to work on and what their weaknesses are.

Usually, we also ask candidates what is most important to them about their job:

- Monetary compensation
- Home/work/life balance
- Culture

We ask what they're looking for in a leader, too, so we can assess whether they'd fit in with our organization.

3. FOLLOW-UP

At the end of the interview, we let the candidate know we'll get back to them quickly. After they leave, everyone confidentially writes down a number between 1 and 5. If the average of those numbers is a 3.5 or higher, we move forward with the hire. At this stage, we consider what's important to them and curate their offer.

What to Offer

Be flexible. Find out what's important to the person you want to hire, and focus on that. If the potential employee cares mostly about compensation, find a pay plan that satisfies them. If healthcare and well-being are priorities, provide them with benefits. If work-life balance is their number-one priority, you need to be okay with flexible work hours.

And don't forget, you need to do all this with HR in mind.

Competitive Compensation

Most traditional dealerships don't offer full benefits. They also don't offer hourly or salary compensation plans—they pay their salespeople commissions only, and their service team is on a flat-rate payment system.

I believe in paying employees either salaries or by the hour because I know people want to feel secure and stable so they can concentrate on their jobs. I don't believe in commission-based or flat-rate pay structures, and we tell all our candidates that. I rely on my managers to ensure they get their jobs done (more on that in future chapters).

We communicate all this upfront, which has made a huge impact on our recruiting efforts. Most dealerships are in desperate need of *good* service techs. We don't have that problem. We have a healthy, happy staff of service techs, all because we pay them by the hour.

Full Benefits

You need to offer *full* benefits to your employees—medical, dental, vision, short- and long-term disability, a 401(k), and paid time off (vacation and sick days).

Research shows that offering comprehensive benefits packages, including medical, dental, vision, disability insurance, a 401(k), and paid time off, significantly enhances employee satisfaction, retention, and productivity. Benefits such as health insurance and retirement plans provide a sense of security and well-being, which contributes to higher job satisfaction and employee engagement. When employees feel valued and supported, they are more likely to be loyal to the company, leading to reduced turnover rates and increased productivity.[12] [13]

Companies that offer robust benefits packages are better positioned to attract top talent. In a competitive job market, having a strong benefits program is essential for demonstrating commitment to employees' well-being and showing that the company cares about employees' personal and professional success. This commitment helps build a positive workplace culture, which in turn fosters employee loyalty and reduces the costs associated with hiring and training new employees.[14]

By investing in comprehensive benefits, dealerships not only enhance their ability to retain valuable employees, but they also create a more motivated, productive, and satisfied workforce. This investment ultimately contributes to the long-term success and stability of the business.

But when offering benefits, make sure they're good. It's almost worse to have bad insurance. If your employee has a challenge at their doctor's office because the insurance you provide only covers a portion of their bill, they're going to be mad at *you*, not the doctors or the rates.

And if they're mad at you, they likely won't be as happy at work.

We don't want our employees to suffer at their doctors' offices. We want that process to be seamless and easy because we want them to feel good and valued.

Traditional dealerships don't offer benefits, which employees often perceive as greedy. "They're just keeping all the money for themselves." Is this the kind of attitude you want from your employees? Do you think it will help or *hurt* your sales?

Flexible Working Hours

We offer all our employees full benefits. We also offer flexible work hours.

Flexible work hours offer a range of benefits that can make a workplace more enjoyable and productive for everyone involved. For employees, having the flexibility to manage their schedules helps them balance work with personal commitments, like picking up kids from school or attending a doctor's appointment. This kind of flexibility can reduce stress and make employees feel more in control of their lives, leading to greater job satisfaction. When people are happy at work, they're more likely to stick around, which means companies spend less time and money hiring and training new employees.

When employees can choose their most productive times to work, they tend to get more done. Some people are morning go-getters, while others hit their stride in the afternoon or evening. Allowing employees to work when they're at their best can lead to higher-quality work and increased productivity. Flexible work hours can also help attract new talent, especially those who value a good work-life balance. In today's job market, many people are looking for roles that offer this kind of flexibility, making it a great perk to offer when trying to stand out as an employer.

For businesses, flexible work arrangements can reduce absenteeism because employees can shift their hours instead of taking full days off for personal matters. This kind of policy shows trust in employees, making them feel more engaged and motivated. Plus, it can save companies money by reducing the need for large office spaces and cutting down on costs associated with strict work schedules, like overtime pay. Offering flexible work hours can create a more positive, productive, and cost-effective workplace where employees feel valued and are eager to contribute.

Ability to Work Remotely

Offering remote work opportunities at my car dealerships has proven to be incredibly beneficial for both my teams and the business. For my teams, having the flexibility to work from home has allowed them to better manage their work-life balance. They don't have to deal with long commutes, which gives them more time to spend with their families or focus on personal activities that help them recharge. This flexibility has significantly reduced stress levels and boosted overall job satisfaction. When my teams feel happier and more engaged, they're more motivated to provide excellent service to our customers, which naturally leads to better sales and customer retention. Plus, when employees are satisfied, they're more likely to stay with us long term, which saves us the hassle and costs associated with high turnover.

From a business perspective, offering remote work has allowed us to tap into a broader talent pool. We're no longer limited to hiring locally; we can recruit the best people for the job, regardless of where they live. This has helped us build a more diverse and skilled team, which is great for bringing fresh ideas and perspectives to the dealership. Additionally, with fewer people needing to work on-site every day, we've been able to cut down on some overhead costs related to maintaining a larger office space. Focusing on results rather than just hours spent in the office has also fostered a more results-driven culture, where the team is more focused on achieving goals rather than just clocking in and out. Overall, embracing remote work has been a win-win, creating a more flexible, inclusive, and productive work environment that benefits both the employees and the dealership.

HIRE AND TRAIN A TEAM OF TULLYS

I first hired Tully when I was the GM at Toyota #1. He followed me when I bought into Toyota #2 and #3.

Tully was my best hire. He quickly picked up on my philosophies, put them into practice, and advocated for them. He believed in the philosophies so much, he sold other staff members on them. It wasn't long before Tully became my best trainer.

I trust that he will teach my philosophies the way I would because he follows my practices. I know exactly how he would handle a challenging situation—he would handle it exactly like I would. Tully has helped me hire and train more people like him, so now I have a whole team of Tullys.

Every car dealership owner, operator, and GM needs a Tully; someone who can be trusted to uphold and train others on their best practices. You need someone who believes in what you do and accurately puts those beliefs into action because you can't be everywhere all at once. You need someone you can rely on to carry the torch in your absence. This is especially true if you oversee multiple stores like I do.

Tully believes in my unorthodox philosophies. All of them. And none are more unorthodox than the next—how my team and I do sales.

CHAPTER 8

HOW WE DO SALES

Philosophy 5

When I first got to Toyota #3, the sales process was very old school. It was heavily focused on traditional methods—phone calls, setting appointments, and trying to get customers into the store. The goal was simple: make the appointment. Get the customer in, and close the sale. But the overall process lacked innovation, efficiency, and a focus on what the customer needed or wanted. The sales closing ratio was pretty low, averaging about 9–10%, and there wasn't much emphasis on building relationships with customers or improving the experience for them.

Fast forward to now, and it's like night and day. We've modernized our approach in almost every aspect. Our current strategy focuses on meeting the customer where they are in their buying journey. Instead of just trying to get them into the store, we equip our team with the tools to pick up where the customer left off online. We offer complete transparency in our quotes, including payment information upfront, even if the customer hasn't explicitly asked for it. This makes a huge difference. Customers appreciate the full picture—it builds trust and makes the process smoother.

As a result, we've seen our closing ratios soar. We're now averaging 14–21%, which is a significant improvement. Our sales consultants are more empowered, customer focused, and ready to offer a seamless experience from start to finish, making both the customer and the team more satisfied with the process.

SALES TEAM DYNAMICS

The sales department is the engine that drives success. The effectiveness of this department determines not only the volume of vehicles sold but also the level of customer satisfaction and loyalty. Our approach to managing the sales department has been shaped by years of experience, focusing on empowerment, training, customer relationship building, technology, adaptation to marketing trends, and a positive work environment to streamline operations.

EMPOWERING THE SALES STAFF

At our dealerships, we don't just guess what cars to stock or how to sell them—we rely on a treasure trove of data to guide every decision. Our inventory lineup isn't just a random assortment but a carefully curated selection based on the latest market trends and customer behaviors. This means when a customer walks in, they see vehicles that align perfectly with what they're looking for. Our sales strategies, too, are tailored and responsive, shaped by real-world data that ensures we're always in sync with what customers expect. This smart use of data keeps us agile, effective, and always ready to deliver exactly what our customers need, making the buying experience not just satisfying but spot-on perfect every time.

It's also spot-on perfect because we empower our sales staff. Empowering them isn't just about training them to handle transactions—it's about instilling confidence and ownership in every step of the sales process. Our sales team doesn't just know the numbers; they live and breathe them. Each team member is equipped to discuss payments, trade-ins, and financing options on the spot, creating an environment where every interaction is seamless and responsive. This approach makes customers feel valued and understood, knowing they're dealing with someone who can address all their needs directly without running to a manager for answers. It's a game changer—both for our staff, who feel more trusted and capable, and for our customers, who experience a level of service that's efficient, transparent, and refreshingly straightforward. The sales team becomes not just sellers but trusted advisors, making the car-buying process smoother, more personalized, and ultimately more satisfying.

TRAINING AND DEVELOPMENT PROGRAMS

Our training programs are designed to equip salespeople with the skills and knowledge they need to excel. New hires undergo a structured onboarding process that includes shadowing of experienced salespeople, role-playing exercises, and extensive product training. This ensures that they are prepared to interact with customers from day one.

Beyond initial training, we offer ongoing professional development opportunities. These include workshops on the latest industry trends, sales strategies, and customer relationship management. We also bring in external experts to provide fresh perspectives and advanced sales techniques. Continuous learning is emphasized to keep our sales team at the top of their game.

When the management team and I noticed that many salespeople were initially resistant to training that took them away from the showroom floor, we emphasized the long-term benefits of continuous learning. By investing in our team's development, we saw significant improvements in their confidence, their customer interactions, and, ultimately, their sales performance.

THE LEGENDARY BEAVER DRAGON

One of the most cherished relationships I've built is with Beaver Dragon, a former racer and extraordinary 85-year-old man who constantly inspires me.

My connection with Beaver began through Heritage Toyota, a dealership owned by a Rolex World Champion race car driver. Beaver wasn't just any racer—he was one of the winningest drivers in the sport and had even competed against my Uncle Vince. When he started sharing stories about those races, it sparked an instant connection.

Over time, our bond grew stronger. Beaver began visiting the dealership regularly, and we hit it off immediately. Today, he buys every car from me and sends countless customers my way, always singing my praises. Our relationship has even extended to his family—his granddaughter works for me remotely. It's a testament to the kind of lasting relationships I strive to build, both in and out of the dealership.

Beaver checks in on my racing regularly, always eager to hear updates and share his wisdom. When he was in the hospital, I checked on him to see how he was doing. He's not just a legend in racing; he's an impressive human being whose friendship I deeply value.

My connection with Beaver goes beyond racing—it's about genuine friendship and mutual respect. This is the kind of connection the leadership team and I want the sales teams to cultivate with their customers. We encourage them to use their personal cell phones so they're always accessible. We tell them, "Make such good friends with your customers that they'll follow you wherever you go." Our goal is for every salesperson to build relationships like the one I have with Beaver.

STRONG CUSTOMER RELATIONSHIPS

Every day, our sales teams manage customer relationships and objections like pros, and they do it with such finesse that it makes us all proud. Their ability to turn a business transaction into a long-term relationship is a cornerstone of our success.

In today's market, building strong customer relationships is more important than ever. Gone are the days when a high-pressure sales pitch would suffice. Customers now seek a consultative approach, where salespeople act as trusted advisors rather than pushy sales agents. This shift requires a deep understanding of customer needs and a genuine commitment to meeting them.

One of the key strategies we implemented was to encourage salespeople to follow up with customers after their purchase. This simple act of reaching out to see how they're enjoying their new vehicle or if they have any questions or concerns can significantly enhance customer loyalty. Our CRM system played a crucial role in this, helping salespeople track and manage their customer interactions effectively.

Handling customer objections effectively is a crucial skill for any salesperson. We train our team to listen actively to customers' concerns, empathize with them, and provide clear, honest responses. Whether it's about pricing, vehicle features, or financing options, addressing objections with confidence and transparency helps build trust and move the sale forward.

During training sessions, we use role-playing scenarios to

practice handling common objections. This helps salespeople develop the skills and confidence needed to navigate challenging conversations and turn potential objections into opportunities.

LEVERAGING TECHNOLOGY

Technology has revolutionized the automotive sales process. From CRM systems to digital marketing tools, technology enables us to streamline operations and provide a better customer experience. For instance, our CRM system allows salespeople to keep detailed records of customer preferences, past interactions, and follow-up schedules, ensuring that no lead is overlooked.

We also embraced digital retailing, which became particularly crucial during the COVID-19 pandemic. Customers could browse our inventory online, schedule test drives, and even complete much of the purchase process from the comfort of their homes. This convenience not only boosted our sales but also enhanced customer satisfaction.

In today's digital age, the integration of digital retail solutions has become crucial for automotive dealerships because it helps them reach a broader audience. Potential customers from outside the immediate geographic area can explore inventory and make purchases online, expanding market reach. This is particularly beneficial during times when physical showroom visits are limited, such as during extreme weather or the COVID-19 pandemic.

For the sales team, digital retail solutions can significantly streamline operations. Automated systems handle routine tasks such as data entry and appointment scheduling, freeing up salespeople to focus on building relationships with customers. Real-time inventory updates and online customer profiles help sales staff stay informed and provide personalized service, improving overall efficiency and effectiveness.

This approach not only enhances the customer buying experience but also streamlines the sales process, making it more efficient and effective.

SMARTPATH

Toyota's SmartPath is revolutionizing the traditional car-buying experience by fully integrating digital tools into the sales process. This state-of-the-art platform empowers salespeople by putting all critical information—such as vehicle specs, pricing options, lease rates, trade-in values, and financing details—directly at their fingertips via tablet or smartphone. Imagine a customer walking in with a vague idea of what they want; within seconds, the salesperson can provide them with a full range of options, from detailed breakdowns of monthly payments to comparisons of similar models. This immediacy not only builds trust but also cuts down the often-dreaded negotiation phase. Customers appreciate this transparency and speed, knowing they're getting precise information without any hidden fees or surprises. The tool also allows salespeople to seamlessly pivot between different scenarios, offering real-time adjustments based on the customers' needs and budget constraints. The days of back-and-forth trips to the manager's desk are over; with SmartPath, the entire transaction feels more fluid, personalized, and customer focused, ultimately leading to higher satisfaction and stronger sales performance.

We've been pioneers in utilizing Toyota's SmartPath, not just as users but as contributors to its evolution. From the very start, we were among the first three dealerships to test this digital retailing tool, providing critical feedback that shaped its features to better align with real-world dealership needs. We recognized the potential of SmartPath to revolutionize the car-buying experience, and our involvement went beyond mere usage—we actively participated in its development. Over time, our sales team has embraced this technology, transforming the customer interaction by providing instant access to detailed vehicle information, pricing, leasing, and financing options. This tool has allowed us to move away from traditional sales tactics and focus on delivering a seamless, transparent, and customer-centric experience. We've seen firsthand how SmartPath empowers our sales staff to make informed decisions without the constant back-and-forth with managers, significantly speeding up the sales process. It's not just a tool for us; it's a game changer that reflects our commitment to innovation and keeping our customers' needs at the forefront of our business strategy.

By embracing digital retail, we not only enhance the customer experience but also ensure that our sales operations remain competitive and adaptable in an increasingly digital world. This integration is a testament to our commitment to innovation and customer satisfaction.

ADAPTING TO MARKET TRENDS

The automotive industry is constantly evolving, and it's crucial for sales departments to stay ahead of market trends. We regularly analyze market data to identify emerging trends and adjust our strategies accordingly. This includes staying updated on new vehicle technologies, changes in consumer preferences, and economic factors that may impact sales.

STAYING UPDATED ON NEW VEHICLE TECHNOLOGIES

Technological advancements in the automotive industry are rapid and impactful. From self-driving capabilities to enhanced safety features and advanced infotainment systems, staying abreast of these developments is essential. Our sales team receives regular briefings and training sessions on the latest vehicle technologies to ensure they can effectively communicate these features to customers. This positions our dealership as a knowledgeable and reliable source of information, enhancing customer trust and satisfaction.

RESPONDING TO CHANGES IN CONSUMER PREFERENCES

Consumer preferences can shift quickly, driven by various factors such as lifestyle changes, environmental concerns, and economic conditions. We closely monitor these shifts through customer feedback, market research, and industry reports. For example, the increasing interest in environmentally friendly vehicles led us to expand our inventory of hybrid and electric vehicles (EVs). Understanding these preferences allows us to stock the right vehicles and tailor our sales strategies to meet customer demands.

ANALYZING ECONOMIC FACTORS

Economic factors such as interest rates, fuel prices, and overall economic health can significantly influence car sales. We keep a close eye on these indicators and adjust our sales tactics accordingly. For instance, during periods of economic uncertainty, we might offer more attractive financing options or focus on promoting vehicles known for their fuel efficiency. By being responsive to the economic climate, we can better serve our customers and maintain steady sales.

THE IMPORTANCE OF A POSITIVE SALES ENVIRONMENT

Creating a positive sales environment is critical for maintaining high morale and motivation among salespeople. A motivated team is not only more productive but also more effective in engaging with customers and closing sales. We foster a culture of collaboration and recognition, ensuring that each team member feels valued and supported. Here are some key strategies we implement to create and maintain a positive sales environment.

FOSTERING COLLABORATION AND TEAMWORK

At our dealership, we emphasize the importance of collaboration and teamwork. Salespeople are encouraged to support and learn from each other, sharing tips, strategies, and experiences. This team-oriented approach creates a supportive environment where everyone is invested in each other's success. It also helps new hires integrate quickly, as they can rely on their more experienced colleagues for guidance and support.

SALES COMPETITIONS AND INCENTIVES

Introducing friendly competition through sales competitions can significantly boost motivation and performance. We regularly organize sales contests with various rewards such as cash bonuses, gift cards, or extra time off. These competitions not only drive sales but also create a fun and dynamic work environment. Salespeople are motivated to push their limits and achieve their best, knowing that their efforts will be recognized and rewarded.

RECOGNITION AND REWARDS

Recognition is a powerful motivator. Our "Salesperson of the Month" award is a prime example of how acknowledging individual achievements can inspire the entire team. This award not only boosts the morale of the top performer but also sets a benchmark for others to strive toward. Public recognition during team meetings and on our dealership's internal communications channels ensures that everyone is aware of the achievement, fostering a culture of excellence.

CREATING A SUPPORTIVE CULTURE

Beyond formal recognition and incentives, creating a genuinely supportive culture is vital. This means fostering an environment where salespeople feel comfortable seeking help, sharing their challenges, and celebrating their successes together. Managers play a crucial role in this by being approachable and providing consistent support and feedback. Regular one-on-one check-ins with team members help managers understand individual needs and provide personalized guidance.

The physical environment of the sales department also plays a role in creating a positive atmosphere. We ensure that the workspace is comfortable, well organized, and equipped with the necessary tools and technology to support our sales team. A pleasant and functional workspace contributes to overall job satisfaction and productivity.

Creating a positive sales environment is essential for maintaining high morale, motivation, and productivity among salespeople. By fostering a culture of collaboration and recognition, holding regular team meetings, organizing sales competitions, and providing consistent support and professional development opportunities, we ensure that our sales team remains engaged and motivated. This positive environment not only enhances individual performance but also contributes to the overall success of the dealership, driving long-term growth and customer satisfaction.

EMPHASIZING INTEGRITY AND TRANSPARENCY

Integrity and transparency are the foundations of our sales philosophy. We believe that being honest and upfront with customers builds trust and leads to long-term relationships. This means providing clear and accurate information about pricing, financing, and vehicle features and never resorting to high-pressure tactics.

A significant change we implemented was transparent pricing. By displaying fair and consistent prices on our vehicles, we eliminated the need for haggling and created a more pleasant buying experience for our customers. This approach has been well received and has contributed to higher customer satisfaction and loyalty.

A dealership's sales team is its heartbeat. The performance of salespeople directly impacts the dealership's bottom line. Therefore, it's essential to cultivate a motivated and well-trained sales force.

Mastering the art of sales in the automotive dealership industry requires a strategic approach that combines training, technology, customer relationship building, and a positive sales environment. By focusing on these key areas, we have created a sales department that not only drives profitability but also enhances customer satisfaction and loyalty. As the industry continues to evolve, our commitment to excellence in sales will ensure our continued success and leadership in the market.

It is a multifaceted endeavor that requires a strategic and holistic approach. By investing in our people, leveraging technology, building strong customer relationships, and creating a positive sales environment, we have established a foundation for long-term success. As we look to the future, our commitment to excellence will guide us in navigating industry changes and maintaining our position as a leader in the market.

Before I stepped in as co-owner, sales at Toyota #3 were managed traditionally, and its numbers were low—it averaged a 9–10% sales closing rate. Revising the dealership's sales processes with the customer and employee experience in mind and getting the team to buy in to the new systems, was a game changer. As of 2024, the average closing rate is higher, ranging from 14–21%.

One of these new systems changed the way Toyota #3 handled lead responses. This philosophy, one of my most unorthodox, is next.

CHAPTER 9

LEAD RESPONSES

Philosophy 6

When I first started at Toyota #2, the approach to handling internet leads was pretty straightforward and traditional but not very effective. The goal was simple: get the customer to come into the store. Whether it was through phone calls or emails, everything revolved around securing an appointment. If there was a phone number, the immediate response was to call—sometimes up to three times—just to try to get the person through the door.

The same went for email leads. Rather than engaging the customer or providing detailed information, the focus was on booking an appointment. The thinking was that once we had them in the store, we could close the deal. But that was the whole problem. It created a narrow and rigid process that didn't take into account what the customer actually wanted or where they were in their buying journey.

At the time, the average closing ratio hovered around 9–10%, which wasn't terrible, but it wasn't great either. When I came on board, I saw the potential to increase that number. Through a more customer-focused strategy, one that met them where they were in their process, we were able to improve that ratio significantly. Now, we're averaging between 14–21% on internet lead conversions, and that's because we started focusing on engaging customers with real information, not just rushing them to an appointment. We turned the entire approach on its head and saw instant results.

TOO MUCH INFORMATION?

The way lead responses are handled in the dealerships I co-own or manage is probably one of my most unorthodox philosophies.

I believe in giving customers the full and complete price of the car *before* they come to the store, without requiring their personal information. My team and I do this either via website or phone—if they visit us online or call into the dealership, they get all the information upfront.

This philosophy is met with a lot of resistance because most traditional dealerships' purpose is to collect the lead's personal information and get them physically in the store. Most will do whatever it takes, including withholding pricing information, until the customer is in the store. A lot of dealership leaders reading this will argue that we give away too much information ahead of time, and these potential customers will take our numbers and shop them around to find a better deal.

Sure, they could do that.

But I argue that if dealerships hide the price or are reluctant to give that information away, the potential customer will view that as distrustful. When they receive pricing upfront, the customer drops their guard.

The proof is in the pudding. When Tully and I implemented my philosophy on lead responses at the store, within weeks sales started increasing like crazy.

HOW TRADITIONAL DEALERSHIPS RESPOND TO LEADS

To make sure we're all on the same page, this is how a lead is generated for a traditional car dealership:

- The customer either calls into the store or goes online to find out information about a car they are interested in. They are only able to get a portion of the information they're looking for upfront.
- If they are online, they submit a request for more information, which includes their personal information.
- If they call into the store, they are told they need to visit in person for pricing. Sometimes, personal information is required at this stage, too, in order to make an appointment.

We don't follow these lead response practices at all. Anyone visiting our websites gets all the pricing information for any car they are interested in upfront. And all of our websites are very easy to navigate and list transparent pricing.

We give the customer *everything* they need to make a purchase decision.

HOW MY TEAM RESPONDS TO LEADS

Anyone who calls into the store gets transparent pricing too. *All* our salespeople have *all* the tools they need to provide these leads with the pricing information requested. They have access to incentives, accurate trade-in values, and warranty costs. This ensures that when a lead interacts with our salespeople over the phone or via email, our salespeople are legitimately ready to help the customer buy because they already have all the information the customer needs.

And everyone knows this works because our stores are consistently in the top three for highest closing rates in the region.

BRAND CLOSE RATE DEALER RANKINGS

	Dealer	Oct 2023 Close Rate (90 Days)		Dealer	Oct 2023 Close Rate (90 Days)
1	Toyota #2	12.8%	10	██████	9.5%
2	██████	12.7%	11	██████	9.3%
3	Toyota #1	11.5%	12	██████	9.0%
4	██████	11.3%	13	██████	8.9%
5	██████	11.1%	14	██████	8.8%
6	██████	10.9%	15	██████	8.8%
7	██████	10.2%	16	██████	8.6%
8	██████	9.9%	17	██████	8.3%
9	██████	9.7%	18	██████	8.3%

Here's how our process breaks down.

STEP 1: IDENTIFY WITH THE CUSTOMER

We always encourage the sales team to put themselves in their customers' shoes when responding to leads. We ask them to think about questions like:

- If you were interested in purchasing a new car, what information would you want to see in an initial quote?
- How much information do you need to make a purchase decision?

The team and I have taken a different approach when it comes to sending quotes to potential customers. Instead of just offering a basic price or answering specific questions, we go above and beyond by providing all the information a customer might need—payments, lease options, financing details, and more—even if they don't ask for it.

Our goal is simple: make the process as seamless and transparent as possible. We don't want customers to have to come back and ask for more information or feel like they're missing something. By giving them everything upfront, we eliminate any friction and make the decision process easier for them.

The response has been overwhelmingly positive. Customers genuinely appreciate this level of transparency and thoroughness. We often hear how thankful they are for making things so easy for them. It's a simple philosophy—give them everything humanly possible—and it builds trust, makes the experience smoother, and ultimately helps us stand out from the competition.

STEP 2: DESIGN THE QUOTE

Everyone on the team is instructed to design the quote exactly like what the lead asked for. They are also trained to give the customer all the information they requested on the phone or over email or text.

Everyone on the sales team is trained to fine-tune their quotes to the needs of the customer too. They know how to answer all their leads' questions and are even equipped to set financing terms.

If the car is no longer available, our salespeople communicate that immediately. They then follow up with details about a similar vehicle we have on the lot or in route from Toyota.

STEP 3: AVOID TEMPLATES

Most dealerships use CRMs, which include templates. We don't use any templates at our stores. All the communication is personalized. We even trust salespeople to use their own phones to communicate with their leads, as long as they input all the information into our CRM so someone can step in to help if needed. This helps establish a trusted relationship between the salesperson and their lead.

Templates aren't used in customer communications at our dealership because they can often come across as robotic and impersonal. When responses sound too much like they're coming from a computer rather than a human, it can alienate customers and fail to build a genuine connection. Centralized business development centers (BDCs) that rely on templates tend to focus solely on getting customers into the store rather than addressing their specific questions or needs. This can be frustrating for customers who are looking for direct, personalized answers, and they may feel like they're not being heard or understood.

BDCs are often designed to provide quick, standardized responses, which may not always offer the detailed information that customers are seeking. In some cases, BDCs are racing to provide quick responses simply to meet manufacturer expectations or quotas rather than truly engaging with the customer. This approach can lead to lower customer satisfaction and missed sales opportunities.

Taking the time to provide personalized, thoughtful responses may take a bit longer, but it significantly improves the chances of converting inquiries into actual sales. Customers appreciate when their concerns are addressed directly and in a manner that feels authentic. By focusing on meaningful engagement rather than quick template responses, dealerships can increase their closing ratios and build stronger relationships with their customers.

STEP 4: MANAGEMENT REVIEW

We also want to make sure the communication between the sales team and their leads is professional, so the sales manager is responsible for reviewing everything sent out (and if a sales manager isn't available, then another salesperson takes a look).

Communication should be easy to read too. Everything that goes out to the customer must be grammatically correct with accurate punctuation and spelling. Reviewing customer communication ahead of time catches these types of errors.

STEP 5: COMMUNICATE WITH THE CUSTOMER

I believe in streamlined, clear communication across the board, whether it's over the phone, email, text, or online chat box (more on how the team works with chats later).

This is especially true for lead responses because clear communication is what's best for everyone, your customers and employees. For the customers, it ensures they get exactly what they want. For the employees, it helps them sell more cars.

Phone

"Hello. I am interested in the white XLE RAV4 listed on your website. Is it still available?"

"Hi! Yes, the car is still available! What can I tell you about it?"

"OK, great. Is the price listed still the same?"

"Yes, all our prices on the website are up to date."

"Last question: I have a car I'd like to trade in, and your website gave me a quote. Will you honor that quote?"

"Yes! We will honor the trade-in price we quoted you on the website. How would you like to see the car?"

Then, whether the customer comes in or not, those quoted prices are honored.

Email

For email responses, our emails usually look a little something like this:

Dear Customer,

Thank you for showing interest in our 2025 Camry XSE—great choice! I wanted to let you know this beauty is still available and sitting on our lot, just waiting for the perfect owner…could it be you?

To sweeten the deal, I'll be sending over some aggressive pricing that's hard to resist, along with a quick personal video so you can get to know both me and your potential new ride. Keep an eye out for it—it's on the way!

I'm here to make this process smooth, fun, and exciting. If you have any questions, big or small, don't hesitate to reach out. Let's make this Camry yours!

Looking forward to connecting with you soon,

Client Advisor

But remember, we don't use templates; each email is tailored to the customer and their needs. It's then reviewed by a manager before it's sent out.

Text

Text messages from our sales team are short and to the point.

> Thank you for inquiring about the XLE RAV4. It's here and available, and I will send pictures and payment and pricing options, if needed. I will follow up with a video of the car and will call you later to make sure you received all the info.

The salesperson then sends the quote and pulls the car out in front of the showroom to take a nice video.

More on the importance of videos in a bit. (And if you want to see a sample video, contact me. I have a ton of resources to help you.)

Also, did you know that text messages have a higher response rate than email?

Text messages boast a 98% open rate compared to only 20% for emails. Additionally, the response rate for SMS messages is significantly higher, with 45% of consumers replying to text messages within 5–10 minutes, while only 6% of emails receive a response. Furthermore, the average response time for a text message is 90 seconds, compared to 90 minutes for an email.[15] [16]

When people contact the store, our sales team typically responds with a text message.

Chat

Chat is another communication tool used by many dealerships, but the end goal is the same as with the other methods we've talked about: to give customers just enough information to get them to visit the store in person.

We don't use chat much in our stores because we can't track the leads. But when we do use it, we approach it exactly the same as we do phone calls, emails, and text messages: we program the chat bot to give the lead all the information they need upfront.

MORE OF THE SECRET SAUCE: VIDEO

Every lead who receives a quote from one of our stores, whether it's via phone call, email, or text message, also receives a short video of the car. This establishes trust between the salesperson and the customer because it confirms the car is still available. It's also an opportunity for the customer to see who they are going to work with to buy their car.

A lot of traditional dealers won't show a video of the car for two reasons:

1. The car is no longer available, but they don't want the customer to know that.
2. They want the customer to come into the store to see it.

We don't work this way because we believe in making things easy for the customer and meeting them where they are.

Once the video is sent, customers receive this follow-up from their salesperson:

> Hello again! You should have received the video and pricing. Please let me know if you have any questions!

VIDEO QUALITY

The quality of your video is critical. No one wants to get motion sickness when watching a video about a car they're thinking about buying. And trust me: you don't want them feeling sick when they're thinking about buying a car from you either.

There is a lot of good video editing software out there that is easy to use and will make your videos enjoyable to watch and look professional. You can easily edit, switch filters, and add music. The quality of your video matters; so does its length. No one wants to watch a video that doesn't give them information quickly. Our attention spans aren't cut out for it anymore. Make sure you're editing your video for length and that you quickly give people the information they're looking for.

Do we include pricing information in the video? Yes, but we give our customers pricing before we send the video. We have found that when we don't give leads the pricing upfront, they only watch the video for a few seconds. They stop watching before they get to pricing. When we give our customers pricing before we send the video, not only do they watch the entire thing, but they do so multiple times and show it to their friends, colleagues, and spouses.

And just like all written correspondence is reviewed before it gets sent out, all videos are too. We don't believe in templates for videos, either, meaning someone other than the salesperson sending the video (ideally, the sales manager) needs to watch it.

LEAD RESPONSE TIME

In the world of automotive sales, lead response time is critical. Data indicates that 78% of customers buy from the first company that responds to their inquiry.[17]

I cannot stress enough how important it is. The wrong timing, and you'll lose the lead. Many dealers try to respond to each lead as quickly as possible—they believe customers want to hear back from them immediately.

But a quick response doesn't necessarily equate to a *quality* response because it doesn't consider the customer and where they are in their car-buying journey.

When a customer inquires about a car, it's typically on a break from their day-to-day life. For example, many people research cars on their lunch break. In between bites, they are visiting your website, calling your store, or emailing for more information.

Our lead response rate at Toyota #2 is consistently between 18% and 20% because we train our sales teams to wait to respond to the lead until about an hour before the lead's *next* break. A lead who has reached out during lunch will likely have time to read a response around 3:00 p.m. Responding too quickly doesn't have as high of a response rate. While quick responses are generally appreciated, there is a fine line between being prompt and being overwhelming.[18]

We are all about quality over quantity. We would rather respond to less leads correctly because it's important to us that our customers have a seamless and positive experience from the very beginning of their car-buying journey. If a salesperson rushes a conversation or cuts corners on a quote, *on some level* the customer will know, and it will impact their car-buying decision.

I'll admit we leave leads on the table with this strategy because sometimes there aren't enough hours in the day for our salespeople to respond to all the leads in our queue correctly.

But I am OK with that. Quality leads are more likely to actually purchase. I know this because our sales keep going up.

To put things into perspective, before I took over as co-owner of Toyota #3, their sales numbers were between 60 and 80 cars a month. Within a few months, they grew to the low to mid100s.

And recently? As of 2024, they were consistently over 200 per month.

MORE LEADS THAN WE CAN HANDLE

Because we are transparent online and over the phone, our stores have a great reputation, and we get more leads than we can handle. Sometimes at the end of the day, the sales team goes home with 20 unanswered leads because we would rather lose business than respond to leads incorrectly.

This one is sometimes a tough pill to swallow—when you're in sales, it's hard to leave money on the table—so the management team and I monitor this practice closely. It's easy to cut corners in general and *especially* when there are too many leads to handle. We want the sales team to handle lead responses the same way *every time*, so we arrange mystery shoppers to audit their work. We record these mystery shopping experiences and share the video during a training session so the whole team can learn and grow.

For all those long-lost leads, they don't go completely forgotten. If a customer's email inquiry goes untouched for 72 hours, our CRM generates an email to determine whether they are still interested. If they are, they go back into the sales system.

GIVE CUSTOMERS ALL THE INFORMATION UPFRONT

When I first changed the lead response practices at Toyota #2, I was met with a lot of resistance.

But that all changed when sales numbers improved.

How I approach lead responses is unorthodox, but it works— our lead response rate is significantly higher than the other stores in the region.

My approach to how dealerships should think about volume versus gross tis unorthodox too. In the next chapter, I'm going to tell you why.

CHAPTER 10

VOLUME VERSUS GROSS

Philosophy 7

I made sure to request Toyota #3's profit statement before making my decision when I began discussions about buying into my first dealership. I wanted to understand the financial health of the business. The high per-vehicle average profit may have scared off some people, but I saw it differently. To me, it was a sign of untapped potential. The dealership had been focusing heavily on maximizing gross profits per vehicle, which meant they were leaving a lot of potential sales on the table by not pursuing volume as aggressively.

This approach—focusing more on gross than volume—was one of the key factors that convinced me to buy in. I knew that if we could shift the strategy slightly to balance volume and gross, the store could truly thrive. That potential for growth and profitability was too good to pass up.

THE TRADITIONAL FOCUS ON GROSS

In the car dealership industry, the debate between focusing on volume versus gross profit per vehicle is perennial. Many dealerships traditionally prioritize gross profit, aiming to maximize the amount of money made on each sale. However, a volume-focused strategy, which emphasizes selling more cars even at lower individual profit margins, can be significantly more profitable in the long run. This chapter explores why a volume-based approach can lead to greater overall success and how it impacts various aspects of dealership operations.

Most dealerships operate with a keen focus on gross profit, which is the total amount of money made per car sold. This metric is straightforward and provides a clear, immediate picture of profitability. For many years, dealerships have relied on this approach to gauge their success. However, this strategy can be limiting and often overlooks the broader opportunities that come with higher sales volumes.

In my experience, focusing solely on gross profit means missing out on a ton of opportunities that come with increased sales volume. For instance, the traditional mindset would hold out for a single $4,000 profit on a Friday rather than making three separate $1,000 sales on Wednesday, Friday, and Saturday. At first glance, the $4,000 might seem superior. However, the volume approach offers several hidden advantages.

UNDERSTANDING THE VOLUME-BASED APPROACH

A volume-based approach shifts the focus from maximizing profit per vehicle to maximizing the number of vehicles sold. While this might seem counterintuitive, especially when compared to the traditional focus on gross, the benefits are substantial. Here's why.

INCREASED TRADE-INS AND ANCILLARY SALES

Selling more cars increases the chances of taking in trade-ins (more on trade-ins and used cars in Philosophy 7). These trade-ins can be refurbished and sold, adding to the dealership's revenue. Additionally, every car sale is an opportunity to sell ancillary products like warranties, GAP insurance, and accessories, which further boost profitability.

For example, each trade-in vehicle presents an opportunity to make additional profit. When a customer trades in their old car, it can be reconditioned and resold. This not only generates profit from the used car sale but also provides another opportunity to sell warranties and service packages, thereby maximizing the revenue from each transaction.

In our service department, we make a significant amount of money on the trades we resell, especially through the service work done on those vehicles. Every time we spend $2,000 servicing a trade-in vehicle, about $1,000 of that turns into profit. It's a major source of revenue because we not only resell the car at a higher value, but we also improve the customer's experience by ensuring they're getting a well-maintained vehicle. By focusing on both quality and efficiency in our service department, we're able to maintain high profitability and keep our inventory in excellent condition for resale.

ENHANCED MARKETING EFFICIENCY

Each vehicle sold acts as a marketing tool. Customers who have positive experiences are likely to recommend the dealership to others. This word-of-mouth marketing is invaluable and significantly reduces the need for expensive advertising campaigns.

In practice, when a customer leaves the dealership satisfied with their purchase, they are more likely to share their experience with friends and family. This organic marketing creates a ripple effect, attracting more customers to the dealership without additional advertising costs. Positive experiences also lead to online reviews and ratings, further enhancing the dealership's reputation and drawing in new customers.

CUSTOMER RETENTION AND LOYALTY

A higher volume of sales increases the dealership's customer base. More customers mean more opportunities to build long-term relationships, resulting in repeat business and higher customer loyalty. These loyal customers are more likely to return for service and maintenance, ensuring a steady revenue stream for the service department.

For instance, every new car sold has the potential to create a lifetime customer. A positive initial sales experience can lead to customers returning for regular maintenance, repairs, and, eventually, another vehicle purchase. This ongoing relationship is beneficial for both the customer, who receives consistent, reliable service, and the dealership, which enjoys a steady stream of repeat business.

THE HIDDEN ADVANTAGES OF VOLUME

Consider this scenario: if a dealership makes $1,000 profit on three separate car sales ($3,000 total) compared to making $4,000 on a single sale, which is better? At first glance, the $4,000 profit might seem superior. However, the volume approach offers several hidden advantages:

1. Trade-Ins: With three sales, there are three opportunities to take in trade-ins, which can be refurbished and sold for addi-

tional profit. This not only boosts used car inventory but also provides multiple touchpoints for generating extra revenue through the reconditioning and resale process, such as service when reconditioning, warranties, and more trades. We also provide a good experience, which increases word-of-mouth leads and reduces advertising costs.

2. Customer Experience: Each sale represents a chance to provide excellent customer service, leading to three different customers potentially spreading positive word-of-mouth. This can significantly enhance the dealership's reputation and attract more customers.

3. Ancillary Sales: Each transaction provides opportunities to sell additional products and services, increasing overall revenue. For instance, every sale is an opportunity to offer financing options, extended warranties, and other add-ons, which can cumulatively add up to a substantial amount of profit.

4. Service Revenue: More cars sold means more vehicles that will eventually need servicing, creating a steady stream of customers for the service department. This ensures that the service bays are always busy, contributing to a stable and reliable source of income.

By focusing on volume, a dealership can create a cycle of continuous engagement and revenue generation. Each customer interaction is an opportunity to build a lasting relationship, enhance the dealership's market presence, and drive long-term profitability.

It took about six months to turn the store around. While we still keep a close eye on gross profits, the primary focus has shifted to volume. The transition was key to driving growth.

I remember when I first reviewed the store's financial statement while sitting on the beach. It was immediately clear that the store was pulling in huge profits but with very low volume. For most, that might be a warning sign, but I saw it as a huge opportunity. They were so focused on gross profits that they were leaving a lot of potential sales on the table, and I knew that by adjusting that focus, we could significantly increase both sales volume and profitability.

THE LONG-TERM BENEFITS

Focusing on volume can also insulate a dealership from market fluctuations. During challenging economic times or periods of high competition, dealerships that rely solely on high gross profits per vehicle may struggle. Those that prioritize volume, though, have a larger customer base and more diverse revenue streams, making them more resilient.

A volume-focused strategy naturally leads to an expanded customer base. Each sale is an opportunity to build a relationship, transforming one-time buyers into long-term clients. A larger customer base provides stability, as these customers are more likely to return for various services, including maintenance, trade-ins, and additional purchases. This expanded network of loyal customers offers a buffer against market downturns, ensuring steady business even when new customer acquisition becomes challenging.

By emphasizing volume, dealerships can diversify their revenue streams. Each car sold is not just a single transaction but a gateway to multiple income avenues. Ancillary products such as extended warranties, financing options, GAP insurance, and accessories contribute significantly to the overall revenue. Additionally, trade-ins taken during these transactions can be refurbished and resold, further boosting profitability. This diversification reduces the reliance on high margins from individual car sales and creates a more stable and predictable revenue flow.

During economic uncertainty, customers become more cautious and price sensitive. Dealerships known for fair pricing and positive customer experiences are more likely to retain their customer bases in these times. A volume-based strategy ensures that the dealership remains competitive in pricing, attracting buyers who might shy away from dealerships with high profit margins per vehicle. Competitive pricing helps maintain sales momentum, even when the economy is sluggish.

A volume-focused approach fosters long-term customer loyalty too. When customers know they can expect fair pricing and a positive experience, they are more likely to return for future needs. This creates a cycle of repeat business that steadily increases profitability over time. Loyal customers are also more likely to refer friends and family, further expanding the dealership's reach without additional marketing expenses.

High sales volume *also* translates to continuous customer engagement. Each transaction, whether it's a sale, service appointment, or trade-in, reinforces the relationship with the customer and increases the likelihood of future business. Regular engagement keeps the dealership top of mind, ensuring that customers think of us first for their automotive needs.

During the COVID-19 pandemic, many dealerships faced inventory shortages and responded by significantly increasing their prices. In contrast, we maintained competitive pricing and focused on volume. This strategy ensured that customers continued to see us as a fair and reliable dealership, leading to sustained sales even during challenging times. By avoiding the temptation to hold out for high gross profits on fewer sales, we maintained our customer base and built a foundation of trust.

Maintaining competitive pricing and focusing on volume not only kept our sales steady during the pandemic but also reinforced our reputation for fairness and reliability. Customers appreciated that we didn't exploit the situation for short-term gains, and this goodwill translated into long-term loyalty and repeat business.

Focusing on volume provides significant long-term benefits for dealerships. It enhances resilience against market fluctuations, diversifies revenue streams, and fosters customer loyalty. By prioritizing fair pricing and positive customer experiences, dealerships can build a stable foundation of repeat business and referrals, ensuring sustained profitability and growth. This volume-based approach is not just about selling more cars; it's about creating lasting relationships and a robust, adaptable business model that can thrive in any economic environment.

OVERCOMING RESISTANCE

Adopting a volume-based approach is not without its challenges. Many salespeople and managers are accustomed to the traditional focus on gross profit and may resist changing their methods. It's crucial to clearly demonstrate the long-term benefits of this strategy and provide continuous support during the transition.

IMPLEMENTING THE VOLUME STRATEGY

Implementing the changes wasn't easy at *any* of my dealerships. At first, it was a real challenge to get the sales consultants fully on board. Their individual unit sales hadn't seen a significant increase, and the shift in focus alone wasn't enough to motivate everyone. The turning point came when I worked with HR to restructure the pay plan. The compensation model had previously been commission-based, meaning the team was focused on gross profits rather than volume. To align their mindset with the new volume-first strategy, we adjusted the pay structure to reward them based on the number of units sold.

Transitioning to a volume-based strategy requires a shift in mindset and operations:

1. Sales Training: Sales staff need to understand the long-term benefits of focusing on volume. Training programs should emphasize building customer relationships and the importance of ancillary sales.
2. Adjusting Pay Plans: Commission structures should reward volume and customer satisfaction rather than just high gross profits. This aligns salespeople's incentives with the dealership's overall strategy.
3. Inventory Management: Maintaining a diverse and well-stocked inventory is crucial to meet customer demands promptly. Efficient inventory management systems can help ensure the right cars are available at the right time.

Shifting to a volume-based strategy can meet resistance, particularly from salespeople accustomed to the traditional focus on gross profit. Overcoming this resistance involves:

- Demonstrating Benefits: Showing clear data and case studies that highlight the long-term profitability of a volume approach can help convince skeptical staff.
- Incentives and Rewards: Implementing incentive programs that reward sales volume and customer satisfaction can motivate salespeople to adopt the new strategy.
- Continuous Support: Providing ongoing training and support helps sales staff adapt to the new approach and succeed in their roles.

Once the pay plan reflected this approach, things started to change. The team realized they could make more money by moving more cars rather than just maximizing profits on each sale. This shift in compensation was crucial—it got the staff to truly embrace the new strategy. As soon as they saw the potential benefits in their paychecks, the momentum picked up, and we started to see real progress. This change was essential for getting the team aligned with the overall goal of increasing volume, and it ultimately led to Toyota #3's success.

A BROAD VISION FOR LONG-TERM SUCCESS

The debate between volume and gross profit is more than just a question of strategy; it reflects a broader vision for long-term success in the automotive dealership industry. By focusing on volume, dealerships can build a larger and more loyal customer base, create diverse revenue streams, and achieve greater overall profitability. This approach requires a shift in mindset and operations but offers substantial rewards for those willing to embrace it. As the industry evolves, a volume-based strategy positions dealerships for sustainable growth and success.

A volume-based approach emphasizes customer relationships by selling more vehicles at competitive prices, attracting a wider range of customers who spread positive word of mouth and return for future needs, ensuring long-term stability.

Focusing on volume taps into multiple revenue streams, as each sale provides opportunities to sell ancillary products and refurbish trade-ins, reducing dependency on high margins from individual car sales.

The cumulative effect of selling more cars results in greater overall profitability, with increased transactions generating higher total revenue and additional sales of ancillary products further boosting the bottom line.

Adopting a volume-based strategy requires a significant shift in mindset and operations, focusing on customer satisfaction and competitive pricing and involving training sales staff and adjusting commission structures to reward volume.

A volume-based strategy positions dealerships to adapt effectively to changing consumer preferences and economic fluctuations, ensuring they thrive even in challenging times by maintaining competitive pricing and focusing on customer experience.

Ultimately, the volume-based approach is about sustainable growth and success. It prioritizes building lasting relationships with customers, creating multiple revenue streams, and achieving overall profitability through increased sales volume. This strategy not only provides immediate financial benefits but also ensures long-term resilience and stability. As the industry continues to evolve, dealerships that embrace a volume-based approach will be better positioned to navigate the challenges and opportunities ahead, securing their future success.

Volume versus gross…and new versus used. In the next chapter, I'm going to tell you my philosophy on new versus used cars and why I prefer the former.

CHAPTER 11

NEW VERSUS USED CARS

Philosophy 8

As a sales manager, I was told to push used cars. The reasoning was simple: new cars would sell themselves thanks to factory incentives and brand reputation. Factory promotions and advertising would drive customers into the dealership for new cars, so our focus should be on maximizing the profits from used vehicles. This approach capitalizes on the higher margins typically associated with used car sales.

This approach always felt counterintuitive to me. I often found myself asking, "How do we get enough used cars if we don't sell new ones?" The answer was either through private sales or auctions, but both options came with their own set of challenges. If it was a private sale, I couldn't help but wonder why someone decided to get rid of their car. Understanding the motivation behind that sale could provide valuable insights into what the customer might want to buy next.

This nagging question sparked a deeper reflection on the entire strategy. It seemed illogical to rely solely on used car acquisitions without considering the larger picture—especially when the quality and quantity of our used inventory depended heavily on trade-ins from new car buyers. Without a steady stream of new car buyers trading in vehicles, we were left with fewer, often lower-quality options. This realization made me question the traditional method and planted the seeds of doubt about the sustainability of the approach I had been taught. It was clear we needed to focus more on new car sales to fuel the trade-in process and ultimately improve our used car inventory.

The idea that new cars would effortlessly drive showroom traffic while we focused on used cars overlooked several critical factors.

1. It ignored the natural life cycle of vehicles and the importance of trade-ins. New car sales generate trade-ins, which are often of higher quality and more desirable than vehicles acquired through auctions. These trade-ins are typically better maintained and come with a known history, making them more attractive to potential buyers and easier to sell at a good margin.

2. The traditional approach underestimated the long-term benefits of customer relationships fostered through new car sales. Customers who buy new cars are more likely to return to the dealership for service and maintenance, taking advantage of warranties and maintenance plans. This ongoing relationship not only drives repeat business but also builds a loyal customer base that is more likely to trade in their old vehicle for another new car from the same dealership.

3. Focusing too heavily on used cars can create a transactional mindset that prioritizes immediate profits over long-term growth. By shifting the focus to new car sales, dealerships can leverage manufacturer incentives, floor plan assistance, and

advertising credits, which can significantly enhance profitability. These incentives are designed to support new car sales and, when effectively utilized, can make new cars a more lucrative option than initially perceived.

As I gained more control and influence within the dealership, I partnered with management to explore and implement a different "new versus used car" strategy. We started by analyzing the financial benefits of new car sales, including manufacturer incentives and the potential for generating high-quality trade-ins. We also considered the broader impact on customer retention and satisfaction. By presenting a compelling case to dealership owners based on data and long-term benefits, we were able to gradually shift the focus of our dealership toward *new* car sales.

I prefer focusing on selling new cars over used ones because acquiring used cars requires additional time and energy. Letting the OEM handle the supply of new vehicles simplifies the process and allows us to focus on sales. By prioritizing new car sales, we naturally increase the intake of used cars through trade-ins. Customers trading in their old vehicles to buy new ones boosts our used car inventory without the need for extra effort, creating a steady flow of both new and used car sales.

ADDRESSING A COMMON MISCONCEPTION

In the automotive dealership world, the debate between focusing on new versus used cars is ongoing. Traditionally, many dealerships have leaned toward selling used cars, often based on the belief that they yield higher profits. My experience has taught me otherwise. I've discovered that emphasizing new cars not only enhances profitability but also aligns better with long-term business goals.

One common misconception is that selling used cars is always more profitable due to higher margins. This belief is rooted in the immediate gross profit per unit, which can indeed appear higher for used vehicles compared to new ones. This narrow focus overlooks the broader financial picture and the additional revenue streams generated through new car sales. When you factor in manufacturer incentives, trade-in opportunities, and long-term service relationships, the profitability of new cars often surpasses that of used cars.

HIDDEN FINANCIAL ADVANTAGES

Are there any advantages? Many. They're hidden.

1. Manufacturer Incentives: New car sales come with various financial incentives from manufacturers, such as floor plan assistance, advertising credits, and stairstep incentives. These incentives are designed to support dealerships in selling new cars and can significantly boost overall profitability. For instance, floor plan assistance helps reduce the cost of financing the inventory, while advertising credits lower marketing expenses. Stairstep incentives, which provide bonuses for reaching certain sales thresholds, can further enhance the dealership's bottom line.

2. Trade-In Opportunities: Approximately 60% of new car buyers trade in their old vehicles. These trade-ins are typically in better condition and have known histories compared to cars purchased at auctions. As a result, they can be resold at higher profit margins. Moreover, the trade-in process itself often leads to higher customer satisfaction, as it provides a seamless transition for the buyer and ensures a steady supply of quality used cars for the dealership.

3. Long-Term Service Relationships: New car buyers are more likely to return to the dealership for warranty services and maintenance plans offered by the manufacturer. This creates a continuous service relationship that generates steady revenue from parts and labor. Regular service visits not only keep the dealership's service bays full but also build a long-term relationship with customers, increasing the likelihood of future vehicle purchases and referrals.

4. Enhance the Dealership's Reputation: Selling new cars enhances the dealership's reputation. New car buyers associate the dealership with the latest models, cutting-edge technology, and the assurance of factory warranties. This association builds trust and reinforces the dealership's image as a reputable and reliable business. Customers perceive a dealership that sells more new cars as more trustworthy and reliable—the idea is that the dealership is doing everything right. This perception is crucial in building a positive brand image and fostering customer loyalty.

5. Attract More New Customers: A dealership known for its robust new car sales can attract a wider customer base. Prospective buyers often look for dealerships with strong reputations for new cars, as it suggests better service, more knowledgeable staff, and a higher likelihood of having the latest models and best deals. This competitive advantage helps the dealership stand out in a crowded market and drives higher sales volumes.

6. Keep Repeat Customers: Customers are more likely to return to a dealership they trust for future purchases and services, leading to a higher rate of repeat business. The positive experience of buying a new car, complete with warranty and maintenance perks, leads to higher customer satisfaction. Satisfied customers are more likely to leave positive reviews, recommend the dealership to friends and family, and return

for future purchases. This cycle of satisfaction and loyalty contributes to the dealership's long-term success.

One illustrative example of this strategy's success is from a month when we sold 210 cars at Toyota #1. Out of these, 65 to 70 were used cars, all sourced from trade-ins. Unlike other dealerships that might rely heavily on auction purchases, our focus on new car sales provided us with a consistent and high-quality supply of used cars. As a result, our profitability soared.

In contrast, another Toyota store in the region, adhering to the old-school philosophy of buying as many used cars as possible at auctions, struggled to match our profitability. Despite selling fewer used cars overall, our store had double the profitability of the other store (we'll keep the name of that store out of this), demonstrating the effectiveness of our approach.

Also, leasing plays a significant role in encouraging customer loyalty because it often requires customers to return to the dealership at the end of the lease term (some manufacturers even mandate that the leased car must be returned to the original selling dealer). This policy benefits the dealership by ensuring a steady supply of high-quality used vehicles, as the returned leased cars become new additions to the used car inventory. It also creates an opportunity to build long-term relationships with customers, as they are more likely to lease or buy from the same dealer again.

THE OPERATIONAL BENEFITS

Our emphasis on new car sales has also streamlined our operations, reducing the complexities and costs associated with auction purchases and reconditioning. Traditionally, buying used cars at auctions involves several hidden costs, including auction fees, transportation expenses, and often significant reconditioning work to bring the vehicles up to retail standards. By focusing on new car sales and generating high-quality trade-ins, we have effectively eliminated these additional costs and streamlined our inventory management.

1. Reduced Acquisition Costs: The costs associated with purchasing auction vehicles can be substantial, including auction fees, transportation logistics, and unpredictable prices. By sourcing our used cars primarily through trade-ins from new car buyers, we avoid these extra expenses. Trade-ins are typically in better condition and come with a known history, reducing the need for extensive reconditioning.

2. Improved Inventory Management: With a steady stream of trade-ins, we maintain a reliable and consistent inventory of used cars. This consistency helps us better predict inventory needs and avoid the fluctuations of auction purchases, allowing us to focus more on selling cars rather than replenishing stock.

3. Streamlined Reconditioning Process: Trade-in vehicles generally require less reconditioning compared to auction-bought cars. They are often better maintained with regular service histories, making them more appealing to buyers. This reduces the time and resources needed to prepare these cars for sale, allowing us to turn around inventory more quickly and efficiently.

The cost savings and efficiencies from focusing on new car sales and trade-ins allow us to invest more in customer service. We can provide better training for our staff, improving their ability to assist customers effectively, which translates to higher-quality service and a more personalized buying experience.

With fewer logistical challenges from auction purchases, our sales processes are more streamlined. Sales staff can focus on building relationships with customers and understanding their needs rather than managing auction acquisitions. This focus enhances the overall sales experience, making it more pleasant and efficient for customers.

Streamlined operations and improved service levels lead to a better customer experience. Buyers appreciate the transparency, quality, and reliability of our inventory, resulting in higher satisfaction rates. Positive feedback and repeat business validate this strategy. Satisfied customers are more likely to return for future purchases and recommend our dealership to others, driving further success.

The strategic shift to focusing on new car sales has significantly improved customer feedback and repeat business. Customers often comment on the ease of the buying process, the quality of the vehicles, and the exceptional service they receive. These positive experiences build loyalty and encourage customers to return for future purchases, whether they are buying a new car, trading in an old one, or seeking service for their vehicles.

OVERCOMING RESISTANCE AND UNLEARNING OLD HABITS

This strategic shift required a change in mindset and approach. To successfully implement it, we focused on comprehensive training for our sales staff. They needed to understand not just the features and benefits of new cars, but also the financial incentives and long-term value they offered to customers.

Salespeople were first trained to highlight the advantages of new cars, such as the latest technology, safety features, and better financing options, including leases. We emphasized building trust through transparent pricing and honest communication, so they were encouraged to present the full picture, including the benefits of factory warranties and maintenance plans. By offering fair trade-in values and explaining the benefits of trading in an old vehicle for a new one, we could increase customer satisfaction and loyalty, we explained.

Next, we presented data highlighting the financial and operational advantages of new car sales, including manufacturer incentives, trade-in profitability, and steady service revenue. This evidence helped make a compelling case for change.

Transitioning to this new strategy wasn't without its challenges. Many salespeople were accustomed to the old philosophy and needed convincing. The traditional approach of prioritizing used car sales was deeply ingrained, and shifting this mindset required a strategic and patient approach.

New salespeople, being more open to change, found it easier to sell new cars due to the inherent advantages such as warranties, new features, and overall reliability. These benefits made it easier to close deals and provided a more satisfying customer experience.

Regular coaching sessions, peer support, and alignment of incentives with new car sales helped experienced salespeople adapt to the new strategy. This ongoing support reinforced the benefits and encouraged a shift in mindset.

Comprehensive training equipped our sales team with the knowledge and skills needed to sell new cars effectively. By demonstrating the clear benefits and providing thorough training, we managed to shift the mindset.

This strategic change not only improved our sales performance but also enhanced customer satisfaction and loyalty, positioning our dealership for long-term success.

THE STRATEGIC CHOICE

The choice between focusing on new versus used cars is more than just a sales strategy; it's about aligning your dealership with long-term profitability and customer satisfaction. This decision impacts every aspect of dealership operations, from financial performance to customer relations. By emphasizing new car sales, dealerships can leverage a range of benefits that extend beyond the immediate profit margins per vehicle. This strategic focus can transform operations, enhance customer experiences, and drive sustainable success.

At each of the Toyota stores I helped turn around, I have seen firsthand how this approach transforms our operations and drives success. By focusing on new car sales, the team and I have been able to tap into manufacturer incentives, generate high-quality trade-ins, and boost service department revenue.

These benefits have not only improved our financial performance but also strengthened our relationships with customers, creating a loyal and satisfied customer base.

Our emphasis on new car sales has also streamlined our operations, reducing the complexities and costs associated with auction purchases and reconditioning. It has allowed us to allocate more resources to customer service and sales processes, enhancing the overall customer experience. The positive feedback and repeat business we receive are testaments to the effectiveness of this strategy.

The future of automotive sales lies in creating seamless, efficient, and customer-centric experiences. In an industry that is constantly evolving, dealerships must adapt to meet changing customer expectations and market dynamics. Focusing on new cars is a pivotal part of this evolution. It aligns with the trend toward transparency, quality, and long-term value, which are increasingly important to today's consumers.

Dealerships that prioritize new car sales will be better positioned to take advantage of technological advancements and shifting consumer preferences. They will be able to offer a superior customer experience characterized by convenience, reliability, and satisfaction. This forward-thinking approach will not only drive immediate sales but also build a strong foundation for sustained growth and success.

The choice between focusing on new versus used cars goes beyond immediate sales tactics; it is a strategic decision that aligns a dealership with long-term profitability and customer satisfaction. By emphasizing new car sales, dealerships can harness manufacturer incentives, secure high-quality trade-ins, enhance service revenue, and build stronger customer relationships. At each of the Toyota dealerships I've helped save, this approach has proven transformative, driving success and positioning us all for a prosperous future in the ever-evolving automotive market. The dealerships that embrace this strategy will lead the industry, delivering exceptional experiences and achieving sustained profitability.

You might not be ready for the next philosophy. I'm going to shock you and argue why you should eliminate your finance department.

CHAPTER 12

ELIMINATE THE FINANCE DEPARTMENT

Philosophy 9

This philosophy is going to shake things up.

The moment I took the helm at Toyota #2, I knew the finance department needed a complete overhaul. Our traditional setup had one finance manager for every 80 cars sold each month—a bottleneck that was frustrating.

My past experiences had taught me the invaluable lesson of efficiency, and with my trusted colleague Tully, we set to work to eliminate the finance department, gradually, a successful strategy management and I had implemented at previous dealerships.

As you imagine, the reaction was mixed. Customers loved it; over time they spent less and less time at the dealership waiting for a finance manager to check them out. The employees took some convincing, but just like every philosophy in this book, once my method proved monetarily beneficial, they came around.

FINANCE DEPARTMENTS: YESTERDAY AND TODAY

Many consumers have a negative perception of the finance department at car dealerships due to several common issues. The process is often viewed as overly complex and confusing, with a bunch of financing options, interest rates, and additional fees that can overwhelm even the most prepared buyer. This complexity can lead to feelings of uncertainty and frustration, as customers may not be fully confident that they are getting a fair deal or completely understand the terms of their agreement.

Consumers frequently experience the finance department as a high-pressure environment. It is not uncommon for customers to feel pushed into accepting extra services or products they might not want, such as extended warranties or GAP insurance. This perception of aggressive upselling can create a sense of distrust, as customers feel that finance managers are more focused on maximizing profits than genuinely helping them.

Another significant issue is the lack of transparency. Many consumers believe that some finance departments are not entirely forthcoming about important details, such as how interest rates are calculated or the actual cost of add-ons. This lack of clear, upfront information can leave customers feeling misled or taken advantage of, further damaging their trust in the dealership.

These negative experiences—stemming from complexity, high-pressure tactics, and a lack of transparency—contribute to a generally distrustful view of the car dealership finance department among consumers.

Traditional car dealerships have heavily relied on finance

departments for several reasons. First, they're a significant profit center. After negotiating the car price, which often leaves minimal profit margins due to competitive pricing, the finance phase allows dealerships to significantly mark up financial products such as extended warranties, GAP insurance, and maintenance plans. These products often carry high margins and represent a substantial portion of a dealership's profitability.

This model relies on finance managers who are skilled in upselling these products during the short window they have with customers, often under high-pressure conditions.

Today, consumer expectations are centered around efficiency and transparency. Modern customers, accustomed to quick and transparent transactions in other aspects of their lives, find the traditional model of car buying—especially the separate finance process—annoying and time-consuming.

By eliminating traditional finance departments and integrating finance roles into the overall sales process, dealerships can offer a more straightforward, less pressurized experience that aligns with modern expectations. This speeds up the transaction process, allowing dealerships to handle a higher volume of sales without bottlenecks, from 80 to more than 200 cars per month.

STEP-BY-STEP ELIMINATION

Are you ready to eliminate your finance department? Great, but do it slowly and step by step. This is important for several reasons:

1. Minimize Disruptions: A sudden removal of the finance department could create significant operational disruptions. By transitioning gradually, the dealership ensures continuous service without adversely impacting the customer experience. This slow change allows the dealership to adjust workflows,

train staff, and implement new processes without the risk of overwhelming employees or reducing sales efficiency.

2. Employee Adjustment: Finance managers and other staff are accustomed to a certain structure and may have specialized in distinct aspects of the sales and finance process. Gradual elimination allows these employees time to adapt to new roles and responsibilities, learn new skills, and adjust to the broader scope of their job. This adjustment period helps retain valuable employees who might otherwise struggle with sudden changes.

3. Testing and Optimization: By implementing changes in stages, the dealership can test new processes and structures to see what works best. This trial-and-error approach allows for fine-tuning procedures and training materials based on real-world feedback and outcomes. Each phase can be evaluated before proceeding to the next.

4. Customer Confidence: Gradual changes help maintain customer confidence and trust. Customers might be wary of abrupt changes, especially in a high-stakes environment like auto sales. Slow and steady restructuring helps prevent customer confusion or dissatisfaction as they grow accustomed to new processes seamlessly integrated into their buying experience.

5. Financial Stability: Each phase of the transition can be monitored for its impact on the dealership's financial health. This ensures that the dealership does not suffer sudden losses in profitability. Gradual changes allow for financial adjustments and new strategy implementations without jeopardizing the dealership's overall economic stability.

6. Staff Buy-In: Gradual change helps in building buy-in from the staff, reducing resistance to new methods. As employees see the benefits of each phase, their support for the transforma-

tion grows, making subsequent changes easier to implement. This phased approach also allows for ongoing training and development, which are crucial for a smooth transition.

By eliminating the finance department slowly and in a structured manner, the dealership ensures a smooth transition that is manageable for staff, comforting for customers, and beneficial for the overall health of the business.

Here are the steps to minimize risks and maximize the impact of the new model.

STEP 1: SEPARATING PAPERWORK FROM SELLING

Initially, the finance managers were swamped, juggling paperwork and product upselling. This not only delayed the process but often soured the customer experience. So we introduced "financial service assistants" (FSAs) whose sole job was to prepare and manage paperwork. This freed up our finance managers to focus on customer interactions and upselling, significantly speeding up the process.

STEP 2: INCORPORATING SALES INTO FINANCE

The next step was to bridge the gap between the sales and finance teams. Instead of having separate roles, sales managers were trained by finance managers to handle both sales and the financial products. This integration meant that a customer dealt with one person throughout their buying journey, fostering stronger rapport and trust.

STEP 3: TRANSITION TO
SALES-DRIVEN FINANCE

Eventually, we transitioned our finance managers to become sales managers, who then took on the role of managing the entire car deal. This change meant that when a customer decided to buy a car, they were presented with additional products seamlessly as part of the sales discussion. They weren't sent to a back office to meet with someone brand new. This approach reduced the shock of separate transactions and allowed us to embed financial products into the car's total price—transparently and efficiently.

IMPACT OF CHANGES ON STAFF

When we implemented the change to eliminate the finance department, the impact on the staff was significant and met with mixed reactions at first. Finance managers, who had previously handled all the financing tasks, had to transition into new roles. The responsibility for managing the financing process was shifted to the sales managers, which meant they had to step out of their offices and become more hands-on in the customer experience. Initially, this was a tough adjustment for some, as they were accustomed to their previous roles. One finance manager ended up leaving, but the others eventually conformed because they found they enjoyed their new roles more than expected.

The pay plans were restructured, with compensation now tied to customer experience rather than simply closing deals. This new model emphasized the importance of customer satisfaction and the overall buying experience, which aligned with the changes we were making across the dealership.

For the salespeople, this shift came with additional responsibility, as they now had more control over the entire sales process, including the financing aspect. However, they quickly realized that this change allowed them to sell more cars because it removed the bottleneck created by the previous finance department. Once they went through the new process a few times, the benefits became clear. The initial resistance gave way to enthusiasm as the entire team saw how the new system improved efficiency and customer satisfaction. Word spread quickly among the staff, and soon, everyone was on board. It was a steamroll effect—once the team experienced the smoother, faster process, they embraced the change, and it ultimately transformed the dealership's operations for the better.

FINANCIAL BENEFITS OF A STREAMLINED APPROACH

Integrating the finance process into the overall sales interaction reduces overhead costs associated with maintaining a separate department. It also decreases the likelihood of sales fallout due to customer fatigue and dissatisfaction with lengthy waiting periods. Financially, while the per-car profit from upsold financial products might decrease slightly, the overall profitability will increase due to higher volumes from quicker sales and enhanced customer loyalty, which often translates into repeat business and referrals.

For salespeople, the elimination of a separate finance manager role meant a significant shift in responsibilities and opportunities. Initially wary of the increased complexity, they soon appreciated the autonomy and trust that came with handling the entire sales process. This approach allowed them to maintain and capitalize on the rapport they built with customers.

Sales managers saw their roles expand to include aspects of financial management. This expansion was a challenge but ultimately led to greater involvement in the dealership's core operations and a better understanding of the nuances of financing. It also provided sales managers with more control over the deal's profitability and customer experience.

Finance managers faced the most significant change, transitioning from specialized roles to more holistic ones. Initially concerned about job security and the loss of specialized tasks, they found that their expertise was not diminished but rather enhanced. They were involved in the entire transaction, which allowed them to use their skills more broadly and contributed to job satisfaction and professional growth.

MERGE YOUR SALES AND FINANCE TEAMS

Removing the finance department was initially met with skepticism but ultimately proved pivotal for our success. Under the new system, the role of the finance manager evolved. These professionals were no longer confined to the back office but were integral to the sales process from start to finish. This shift not only preserved jobs but enhanced them, aligning pay structures with overall deal profitability rather than isolated upsells.

And it removed bottlenecks. Because everyone was given the tools to sell cars from start to finish, we were able to sell more cars.

The transformation of the finance department was a strategic move toward a more integrated, customer-focused business model, and it has proven to be financially beneficial. By focusing on the overall volume and customer experience rather than per-car profitability, we not only increased our sales but also fostered a more transparent and trustworthy environment.

Transforming the finance department was not merely an operational change but a cultural shift toward better service, faster transactions and a more integrated team approach.

What's next? Philosophy 10: Captive Warranty Versus Aftermarket.

CHAPTER 13

CAPTIVE WARRANTY VERSUS AFTERMARKET

Philosophy 10

When I took over operations at Toyota #3, the dealership sold both captive and aftermarket warranties, but the limitations aftermarket warranties put on sales were impossible to ignore.

When we were selling both captive and aftermarket warranties, we quickly noticed some key differences in how they impacted our business and customer satisfaction. While aftermarket warranties were initially appealing—they were cheaper, and we were able to make more per warranty sale—they came with a host of problems. Customers who traveled and tried to get repairs at other stores often ran into roadblocks with these warranties.

The result?

Frustrated customers and a low warranty penetration rate, meaning we weren't selling as many warranties overall.

That's when we made the switch to factory, captive warranties, and everything changed. Not only did our warranty penetration rate improve, but we also kept our service and repairs in-house. With captive warranties, customers are more likely to return to our dealership for their service needs, boosting retention and increasing satisfaction across the board. While aftermarket warranties can be cashed in at multiple locations, captive warranties ensure that customers come back to us, creating long-term loyalty and stronger relationships.

Convincing my partner to make the switch wasn't easy, but I knew it would be more profitable in the long run. Aftermarket warranties might make more money upfront, but the captive warranties gave us more volume, higher retention rates, and, ultimately, greater customer satisfaction. And the numbers didn't lie—once we fully embraced this strategy, it became clear that we were building something stronger and more sustainable.

TRADITIONAL WARRANTY MODELS: THE FINANCIAL APPEAL

Traditionally, dealerships have leaned toward selling aftermarket warranties for several reasons:

1. These warranties often come with lucrative reinsurance programs, allowing dealers to retain a significant portion of the warranty cost if the warranty is unclaimed.
2. This model is financially attractive because it directly boosts profitability per car sold through high-margin warranty products.
3. The administrative fees associated with these aftermarket pro-

grams are generally lower, presenting an immediate financial benefit to the dealership.

But using aftermarket warranties often overlooks the customer's best interests and the dealership's long-term reputation. Aftermarket warranties can be restrictive, covering fewer scenarios and requiring customers to pay upfront for services, only to be reimbursed later. This degrades trust and customer satisfaction, which are crucial for repeat business and long-term success.

If we were going to make a significant impact, we needed to shift our focus to captive warranties.

WHY CAPTIVE WARRANTIES?

For the most part, we *only* sell captive warranties. In the past, I have sold both captive *and* aftermarket warranties, but I avoid that whenever I can now. Captive warranties make the dealership more money (we sell more of them), *and* our customers are happy (they get what they paid for). I can't say the same for aftermarket warranties.

Customers who buy aftermarket warranties often run into problems that can make the whole process more of a hassle than they expected. These warranties aren't always accepted by dealerships, meaning customers might have to find a different place to get their car serviced. Even when the warranty is accepted, customers usually have to pay for repairs upfront and then deal with the headache of getting reimbursed, which can involve lots of paperwork and back-and-forth with the warranty company.

On top of that, aftermarket warranties often have limited coverage, and many customers don't realize what's not covered until they try to make a claim. This can lead to unexpected out-of-pocket expenses and frustration. All these hassles make aftermarket warranties feel less like a benefit and more like a burden.

And disappointed customers rarely become customers for life.

When we switched to captive warranties, the response was overwhelmingly positive. Employees immediately embraced the change, as it simplified the process and reduced the hassle associated with aftermarket warranties. Customers appreciated the transparency and ease of dealing directly with the dealership for warranty services. This approach improved overall satisfaction, as it eliminated the common frustrations customers faced with third-party warranty providers, such as limited coverage and reimbursement delays. The seamless integration of captive warranties enhanced trust and strengthened the relationship between the dealership and the customers.

Aftermarket warranties may seem appealing at first glance due to their lower upfront cost. For example, a 5-year, 60,000-mile warranty for a Toyota Camry from the manufacturer might cost around $1,500, whereas a third-party warranty could be priced closer to $1,000. While this might save money in the short term, it often leads to more expenses and a worse experience in the long run.

One of the key drawbacks is that aftermarket warranties are not always accepted at all dealerships, especially those authorized by the car's manufacturer. This means that a customer with a third-party warranty might face difficulties if they need service outside of their local area or on the road. If they go to a dealership that doesn't honor the warranty, the customer may have to pay out of pocket for repairs and later seek reimbursement, creating hassle and frustration.

Additionally, aftermarket warranties are not backed by the manufacturer, leading to lower trust among customers. People are generally more comfortable purchasing a warranty directly from the dealership, knowing it's supported by the brand that made their vehicle. This also impacts service department revenue—if a customer has a manufacturer's warranty, they are likely to return to the dealership for repairs, generating more business. On the other hand, if a Toyota owner has a third-party warranty and ends up at a dealership that doesn't accept it, the dealership that sold the car loses both that service revenue and potentially the customer's long-term business.

In the long run, while selling third-party warranties might seem profitable initially, the lack of universal coverage and the risk of frustrating customer experiences make these warranties harder to sell and less beneficial to both the dealership and the customer.

Here are all the reasons I prefer captive warranties.

BACKED BY THE MANUFACTURER

Captive warranties are backed by the manufacturer, so they naturally instill greater confidence among buyers because they are perceived as more comprehensive and reliable, and they directly reflect the manufacturer's commitment to the vehicle. Customers are more likely to feel confident that the warranty is comprehensive and specifically tailored to their vehicle—it helps reassure them that any necessary repairs or services will be handled correctly with genuine parts and qualified service. This increased trust leads to higher customer satisfaction, as buyers feel more secure in their purchase.

SIMPLIFIES SALES

Selling only captive warranties simplifies the sales process. Salespeople and finance managers don't need to explain the nuances of multiple warranty providers or compare different plans' benefits and drawbacks. This simplicity makes it easier for them to understand and promote the product, reducing training costs and time.

Think about it from the customer's perspective: if you were buying a Honda generator, would you feel more comfortable purchasing a warranty directly from Honda or choosing a warranty offered by a company like Geico that covers various products? Most customers prefer the peace of mind that comes with a warranty from the manufacturer itself, as it is designed specifically for that product and often provides more comprehensive coverage.

ALIGN WITH THE DEALERSHIP'S BRAND

Because the warranties are factory backed, sales personnel can offer them confidently, knowing they align with the vehicle's brand and quality standards. This alignment helps build a strong brand identity, differentiating the dealership in a competitive market. It also eliminates confusion and mistrust during a sales process that, with too many choices, can easily become overwhelming. Selling captive warranties reinforces the dealership's brand alignment and reputation as a trustworthy and customer-focused business, which builds a stronger rapport with customers.

FINANCIAL INSTITUTIONS LOVE THEM

Banks and other financial institutions often view captive warranties more favorably, which can facilitate financing approvals and create smoother transactional experiences for customers. Banks and other lending institutions often prefer dealing with captive warranties because they perceive these warranties as more secure and reliable. This preference can lead to easier and more favorable financing arrangements for customers and smoother and faster sales transactions. Deals close quicker, and the likelihood of upselling higher-priced vehicles or additional features increases.

LONG-TERM FINANCIAL BENEFITS

Although the immediate financial gains from selling captive warranties might seem lower compared to aftermarket options, the long-term benefits—such as higher customer retention, repeat sales, and enhanced dealership reputation—outweigh the initial profit margin from aftermarket warranties. The immediate profit per warranty sold might be lower with captive warranties compared to aftermarket warranties (due to potentially lower commissions or fees), but the long-term financial benefits are substantial—increased customer loyalty, repeat business, and referrals—and contribute to sustained revenue growth. Satisfied customers are more likely to return for maintenance and repairs, too, boosting the dealership's service department revenue.

REGULATORY COMPLIANCE AND LESS RISK

Captive warranties usually comply seamlessly with any legal requirements or manufacturer guidelines, reducing the risk of regulatory issues. They also lower the dealership's risk by ensuring warranty claims are supported and managed by the manufacturer. This avoids disputes with warranty providers or customers over coverage issues.

The CFPB (Consumer Financial Protection Bureau) has brought attention to issues within the car dealership industry, particularly around extended warranties, price gouging, and negotiation practices. For example, if two customers buy the same car but are charged different prices for the same warranty, this raises concerns about fairness and discrimination. Although existing laws allow for negotiation, the legal landscape is complex. To navigate this, management and I instruct the staff to be transparent and fair, setting consistent pricing and ensuring customers understand what they are buying to avoid potential legal issues.

RESISTANCE, CHALLENGES, AND CONCERNS

The staff immediately took to the new approach because it simplified the sales process. It became easier for them to sell captive warranties because they could confidently back the product, knowing it came from the dealership and the manufacturer. The customers appreciated this as well, since they felt supported, understanding that their warranty was not only reliable but also came directly from a trusted source.

Convincing my partner to embrace this new approach, however, was one of the more challenging parts of the transition. He was skeptical at first, concerned about whether this shift would lead to a decrease in profits. But we actually sold more warranties and cars by focusing on providing customers with trusted, dealership-backed products, and we saw an increase in profit margins, particularly through higher volume. The combination of staff enthusiasm, customer satisfaction, and the overall increase in volume proved the model was not only sustainable but a winning strategy.

Eliminating aftermarket warranties transformed business operations at the store. We attracted more customers looking for reliable and trustworthy service when we improved our reputation by aligning more closely with manufacturers. This shift also simplified our internal processes, allowing our sales team to focus on ensuring that each customer was satisfied and more likely to return.

The change *was* a bit tough on the finance team. Finance managers experienced perhaps the most significant shift in their roles.

Initially, there was concern and resistance among them, primarily because they were accustomed to the high profit margins and incentives (which the warranty company often mailed to their houses) associated with aftermarket warranties. These warranties allowed finance managers to significantly boost their earnings based on upsells, so they saw the switch to captive warranties, which generally offer lower commission rates, as a potential cut in their personal income.

As the transition progressed, though, and the benefits of a simplified, more customer-centric approach became apparent, finance managers began to appreciate the change. They found that the streamlined process led to quicker deal closures and more satisfied customers, which in turn led to higher overall sales volumes. This increase in volume often compensated for the lower individual commission on captive warranties.

Also, the clearer, more transparent selling process reduced the stress and ethical dilemmas involved in pushing harder-to-justify aftermarket products. Aftermarket warranty companies can create ethical dilemmas because they often sell products that do not provide comprehensive coverage, leading to potential conflicts of interest and customer dissatisfaction. These companies may offer warranties that do not cover all the components or types of repairs that a manufacturer's warranty does. As a result, customers might purchase these warranties believing they are fully protected, only to discover later that certain parts or repairs are excluded, leading to unexpected out-of-pocket expenses.

Sales managers initially faced challenges with the new approach, particularly in adapting to and overseeing a different sales strategy. They were responsible for retraining their teams, aligning sales tactics with the new warranty offerings, and ensuring their salespeople were comfortable and proficient in explaining the benefits of captive warranties to customers.

The consistency of offering only captive warranties simplified training requirements and reduced confusion, among both the sales staff and customers. Over time, sales managers noticed an improvement in team morale and customer feedback, leading to a more cohesive environment and higher sales volumes.

Salespeople, who are often on the front lines of customer interaction, initially resisted the change due to similar concerns about reduced commissions. They were used to the flexibility of offering a range of products, which allowed them to tailor deals more creatively. The shift to only selling captive warranties seemed limiting at first.

But as they adjusted, they began to see the benefits of easier sales processes and increased customer trust. The clarity of offering a single, straightforward warranty option made it easier for them to build trust with customers. They found that customers were less guarded, as there was no fear of being upsold on unnecessary extras. This led to better customer relationships, repeat business, and invaluable referrals.

EXCLUSIVELY SELL CAPTIVE WARRANTIES

No one at Toyota #3 was excited about the plan to exclusively sell captive warranties, but the long-term benefits became clear over time: sales and customer satisfaction increased.

And as the dealership's reputation for honesty and customer focus strengthened, so did the morale and job satisfaction among the staff, who appreciated working in an environment that valued ethical sales practices and customer satisfaction above short-term gains.

Choosing to sell captive warranties exclusively was not merely a financial decision—it was a strategic move toward building a sustainable business. It aligns with a long-term vision where customer trust, repeat business, and brand loyalty drive profitability, not just individual transactions. In a competitive market, this philosophy sets us apart, ensuring that our dealership not only survives but thrives by selling good products and putting customers first.

By focusing on what truly benefits the customer, dealerships can foster a loyal customer base that values integrity and transparency—qualities that are indispensable today.

Speaking of the opposite of integrity and transparency, did you know that many *many* dealerships mark up loan rates?

CHAPTER 14

RATE MARKUP

Philosophy 11

In November 2008, as the nation watched Barack Obama win the presidency, a sense of change swept through various industries, particularly automotive. Obamas administration introduced the CFPB, aimed squarely at eliminating financial malpractices affecting consumers. This was especially relevant to auto dealerships and their common practice of marking up interest rates on auto loans.

I remember the day we first heard whispers of these impending regulations. I was in my office, the autumn sunlight barely filtering through the blinds, when I got a call from the district financial manager at Toyota Financial. He shared the news of the CFPB's focus on auto dealerships, warning of an incoming change. Knowing the potential impact of this regulatory spotlight, I immediately scheduled a meeting with our dealership owner. My pitch was straightforward yet controversial: eliminate interest rate markups entirely. It was a proactive measure intended to position us ahead of the regulatory curve and redefine our business ethos. After a lengthy discussion, in which I highlighted both the ethical and long-term business advantages, the owner hesitantly gave the green light.

TRANSFORMING OUR BUSINESS MODEL: A SHIFT TO TRANSPARENCY

The decision to remove interest rate markups was massive. Initially, there was substantial resistance from the finance department, who were accustomed to the easy profits derived from these markups.

But markup was pure profit for the dealership and a significant financial burden on our customers, a message I personally communicated to our dealership staff.

I then spearheaded an intensive training program for our finance managers, reorienting them from relying on interest rates to focusing on selling value-added products like extended warranties and GAP insurance. The transition wasn't smooth, but as the months passed, a remarkable transformation unfolded. Our sales team began to excel at explaining the benefits of these products, leading to a substantial increase in warranty sales. Our profitability soared, and our customer satisfaction ratings followed suit. Within a year, our dealership was recognized with Toyota's Insignia Award for being in the top 5 dealers on the East Coast in product penetration—a testament to our renewed focus on customer value over dealership profit.

We have now won the award 5 years in a row.

MY STANCE AGAINST INTEREST RATE MARKUPS

From the very beginning of my career in the auto industry, I have disliked the practice of interest rate markups. To me, this tactic is not just a minor misstep in dealership operations; it represents a fundamental breach of the trust that should exist between a dealer and their customers. When I think about marking up interest rates, I see it as a way to increase profits by exploiting customers' financial ignorance; it goes against everything I believe in as a business owner and as an advocate for consumer rights.

Interest rate markups are essentially a hidden tax on the uninformed. They target those who may not have the resources to understand the finer details of auto financing. This practice allows dealerships to inflate the cost of loans covertly, which means customers end up paying significantly more over the life of their loan. The extra profit that dealers earn from these markups comes directly out of the pockets of the hardworking individuals who often can least afford it.

This tactic also has a cascading effect on the customer's ability to purchase additional beneficial products like extended warranties and service packages. By artificially inflating the interest rate, we reduce the financial room customers have to protect their investments properly. This is bad business—our role as dealers is to help customers make informed decisions that enhance their long-term satisfaction and safety, not to manipulate them for extra profit.

I've lay awake countless nights, troubled by the industry standard practices that put profits before people. But my team and I chose a different path. We removed interest rate markups entirely, focusing instead on transparent pricing and genuine customer service. The result?

Our customer satisfaction soared, and so did our profits—ethically.

This approach didn't only improve our bottom line; it fundamentally changed the way we did business, aligning our success with the satisfaction and trust of our customers.

This stance against interest rate markups isn't just a part of our business model; it's a crusade against the industry norm. We prove every day that you can succeed spectacularly in the auto industry without compromising ethical standards. Every car that leaves our lot with a satisfied customer behind the wheel stands as a testament to our commitment to fairness and transparency. We have chosen to be a beacon of honesty and integrity, and I am immensely proud of that.

THE IMPACT OF REMOVING INTEREST RATE MARKUPS

The decision to remove interest rate markups fundamentally transformed the dynamics and operational strategies within our dealership. This change not only aligned with emerging regulatory pressures but also significantly influenced the roles and performances of our salespeople, sales managers, and finance managers.

IMPACT ON SALESPEOPLE

The removal of interest rate markups revolutionized the automotive sales landscape, compelling salespeople to shift from relying on financial incentives to honing their product knowledge and selling skills. Here's how they were impacted:

1. Enhanced Product Knowledge and Selling Skills: With the removal of interest rate markups, salespeople could no longer lean on financial gimmicks to close deals. Instead, they needed to deepen their understanding of the vehicles and associated products. This shift demanded a higher level of professionalism and product expertise, as they now had to articulate the intrinsic value of products and services, focusing on features, benefits, and the long-term advantages of owning a well-covered vehicle.

2. Building Trust with Customers: Salespeople found that transparent pricing and financing options significantly enhanced trust with customers. This trust was crucial in fostering longer-term relationships, leading to higher customer retention rates and referrals. The honest approach allowed salespeople to engage more openly with customers, setting a clear and ethical foundation for each interaction.

This transformation not only elevated the professionalism of salespeople but also built stronger, trust-based relationships with customers, driving long-term loyalty and success for the dealership.

IMPACT ON SALES MANAGERS

The introduction of the no-markup policy necessitated a significant shift in sales strategy and training for sales managers, pushing them to adopt a more ethical and customer-focused approach. Here's how they were impacted:

1. Shift in Sales Strategy and Training: Sales managers had to overhaul their training programs to adapt to the new no-markup policy. Training sessions now emphasized ethical sales techniques and focused on educating the team about the importance of transparency and customer service. Sales managers also developed new evaluation metrics that prioritized customer satisfaction and product penetration over mere sales volume.

2. Managing Change and Employee Adaptation: Sales managers played a crucial role in managing the change within the sales team. They had to ensure that all members were on board with the new approach, mitigating resistance and fostering a culture

of adaptation. This often involved one-on-one coaching and the development of incentive programs that rewarded ethical selling and high customer satisfaction scores.

Through these efforts, sales managers not only managed to navigate the transition smoothly but also cultivated a more adaptive and customer-centric sales team, ultimately enhancing the dealership's reputation and performance.

IMPACT ON FINANCE MANAGERS

The elimination of interest rate markups brought about a substantial change in the responsibilities of finance managers, steering their focus toward promoting value-added products. This was the impact:

1. Focus on Value-Added Products: Finance managers experienced a significant shift in their role, moving away from leveraging interest rate differentials as a primary profit generator. Instead, they focused on promoting value-added products such as extended warranties, maintenance packages, and GAP insurance. This shift not only compensated for the loss of revenue from rate markups but also aligned better with customer interests, leading to increased uptake of these products.

2. Enhanced Compliance and Reduced Legal Risks: By removing interest rate markups, finance managers found themselves operating in a more compliant environment, reducing the dealership's exposure to legal risks associated with discriminatory lending practices. This change necessitated a thorough understanding of new compliance requirements and led to the implementation of stricter controls and audits to ensure adherence.

This strategic shift not only compensated for the lost revenue from interest rate markups but also fostered a more compliant and customer-centric environment, significantly reducing legal risks and enhancing overall dealership performance.

The elimination of interest rate markups marked a pivotal shift in the operational ethos of our dealership. It challenged our team to improve their skills, focus on genuine customer benefits, and operate within a framework of heightened ethical standards. The overall impact was incredibly positive, leading to improved customer loyalty, better team morale, and a stronger market position. This transformation illustrated that integrity and success in the automotive industry are not mutually exclusive but are, in fact, synergistic.

LEGAL REPERCUSSIONS AND ETHICAL CONSIDERATIONS

The legal landscape regarding interest rate markups was, and remains, fraught with peril. The practice, while common, often skirted the edges of discrimination and unfair pricing. Several dealerships across the country faced class action lawsuits, hefty fines, and damaging public relations crises when their markup practices came to light. In our case, committing to transparency not only safeguarded us against such legal battles but also enhanced our reputation in the community.

As a dealership, our goal shifted to fostering long-lasting relationships with our customers, which was incompatible with interest rate mark-ups. By eliminating these markups, we ensured that our customers received fair loan rates, improving their trust in our dealership and increasing their likelihood of returning for future purchases.

A CALL FOR INDUSTRYWIDE CHANGE

Reflecting on the journey, the removal of interest rate markups at our dealership not only aligned with the changing regulatory environment but also set a new standard for ethical practices in the auto sales industry. It showed conclusively that a dealership could thrive without resorting to interest rate markups.

The path we chose wasn't easy, but it was right. My hope is that our story serves as a catalyst for change across the industry.

The automotive sales landscape is evolving, and dealerships that anticipate and adapt to these changes, prioritizing transparency and customer welfare, will not only meet the future prepared but will lead it.

CHAPTER 15

CREATE A ONE-TOUCH EXPERIENCE

Philosophy 12

During my tenure as the GM at Toyota #1, I remember a time when Ted, an employee in our BDC department, built a strong rapport with a customer over the phone. The customer, feeling confident and valued, decided to visit the dealership to finalize her purchase. When she got there, she specifically asked for Ted, the young man she had spoken with, only to be redirected to a salesperson. Her visible disappointment was impossible to miss. She had invested time and emotion into her initial interaction, and now she was forced to start over with someone new and repeat her story and preferences. This not only broke the trust she had built, but it also wasted her time.

Seeing her lose her enthusiasm and her shoulders drop was a revelation for me. It became clear that customers value consistency and continuity in their interactions—they want to feel understood and appreciated throughout the entire buying process, not just at the beginning. This incident highlighted a significant gap in our process and got me to rethink how we could better serve our customers by minimizing these disruptive handoffs.

The solution was the implementation of a one-touch experience. (The one touch approach isn't original—it's a concept used by many different dealerships.) By assigning a single representative to manage the customer's journey from start to finish, we could ensure that the trust and rapport built during the initial contact were maintained throughout the entire process.

This approach not only streamlined our operations but also significantly enhanced the customer experience and led to higher satisfaction and loyalty.

MINIMIZE TOUCHPOINTS

In the ever-evolving landscape of automotive sales, one constant remains: the customer experience is paramount. To thrive in this competitive environment, dealerships must adapt and innovate, prioritizing efficiency and customer satisfaction. My approach—the implementation of a one-touch experience for car buyers—has proven successful. This philosophy minimizes the number of touchpoints for a customer, builds stronger relationships, and enhances their overall experience.

Customers value their time and seek convenience in their interactions. Traditional dealership models often require customers to interact with multiple departments and personnel (BDC, sales, finance, etc.), leading to frustration and inefficiency.

The one-touch experience aims to address these pain points by ensuring that a single individual manages the customer's journey from start to finish. This approach eliminates the need for customers to repeat their stories or wait for different departments to communicate, significantly reducing their frustration and saving them valuable time.

At our dealership, we began by rethinking the entire customer journey. When a customer expresses interest in purchasing a vehicle, they are paired with one representative who handles everything from the initial inquiry to the final sale and delivery. This representative is trained to manage every aspect of the transaction, ensuring a seamless and efficient process.

THE BENEFITS OF A ONE-TOUCH SYSTEM

We saw significant improvements in customer satisfaction and operational efficiency after implementing the one-touch system at Toyota #1. Customers no longer faced multiple handoffs and received consistent, high-quality service from start to finish.

Here are some specific benefits we observed:

1. Enhanced Efficiency: Reducing the number of handoffs made the sales process significantly faster. Customers no longer had to wait for different departments to communicate, and their questions and concerns were addressed promptly by their dedicated representative.
2. Improved Customer Satisfaction: The continuity of dealing with a single representative built stronger relationships and trust. Customers appreciated not having to repeat themselves and enjoyed a more personalized experience.
3. Consistency in Service: Each representative was fully equipped to handle all aspects of the transaction, ensuring consistent service quality. This approach also simplified training and staff utilization, as team members were skilled in multiple areas.
4. Cost Savings: Streamlining the process and reducing the

number of specialized roles also led to cost savings. We could allocate resources more effectively and manage our payroll more efficiently.

5. Reduced Bottlenecks: With fewer specialized roles, the dealership became more flexible, and customer wait times decreased (they spent about 25–30 minutes, on average, on paperwork). If a team member called out sick or was on vacation, others could seamlessly step in without disrupting the customer experience. This flexibility ensured our operations ran smoothly and efficiently. Before the finance department was eliminated, there was one finance manager for roughly every 60 cars sold, which created a major bottleneck.

Consider this scenario: Customer A is ready to buy a car, so the finance manager starts the paperwork, which takes about an hour to complete. Meanwhile, Customer B commits to purchasing a vehicle 10 minutes later, followed by Customer C, who commits 10 minutes after that. This creates a backlog, with Customer C having to wait up to two hours to finalize their purchase. In contrast, with my system, everyone is trained to handle the entire process efficiently, ensuring that customers are done within 20–30 minutes.

My approach not only enhanced the customer experience but also increased the number of vehicles we could service each day, driving profitability and growth.

STREAMLINING THE PROCESS

To implement the one-touch approach, we had to overcome several traditional dealership practices. Typically, customers were handed off multiple times: from the BDC department to a salesperson, then to a finance manager, and finally to a delivery specialist. Each handoff required customers to restate their needs and preferences.

To address this, we redesigned our workflow so that the initial representative who engaged with the customer would guide them through the entire buying process. This meant that the same person who answered their initial inquiry would also assist them in choosing a vehicle, handling financing, finalizing the sale, and handing off the car. If the customer wanted an in-depth rundown of all the car's bells and whistles, the same person would handle that too. This continuity ensured that customers felt valued and understood at every step.

I'm also a big fan of at-home car delivery, when it suits the customer. At Toyota #3, we deliver 60–70% of all cars to customers' homes rather than having them come to the store. In contrast, at one of our other locations, we only deliver about 5% of cars. This difference is because that store is located in a metro area, making it easy for people to visit the dealership in person. The varying percentages reflect the differing customer preferences and logistical convenience between the two locations.

In a traditional setup, a finance manager might require customers to visit the dealership in person to finalize their paperwork and purchase. However, with the one-touch system, this need for in-person visits is eliminated. Instead, everything can be handled remotely, allowing for a more convenient process where customers can complete their purchase from home, including having the car delivered directly to them. This approach streamlines the buying experience, saving time for both the dealership and the customer.

Implementing a one-touch system required comprehensive training for our staff, which was hard work. Instead of being specialists in isolated functions such as sales, financing, and delivery, representatives became well-rounded experts capable of managing the entire customer journey. Each team member needed to be proficient in various aspects of the sale, from understanding vehicle features and financing options to completing paperwork and conducting the final vehicle delivery. This cross-functional training was essential to providing a seamless experience for the customer.

(This process wasn't easy—it took us a long time to figure it out and manage—but it was worth the hard work. The gains did come.)

Consider a customer interested in a new car. Under the one-touch model, they interact with one representative who can:

- Discuss their needs and preferences. The representative begins by engaging with the customer to understand their specific requirements, preferences, and budget. This initial conversation is crucial for building rapport and setting the foundation for a positive experience. The representative listens attentively, asking relevant questions to gather all necessary information.
- Help them choose the right vehicle. With a clear understanding of the customer's needs, the representative then guides them through the available options. They provide detailed information about each vehicle, highlighting features and benefits that align with the customer's preferences. This personalized approach helps customers feel confident in their decision-making process.
- Handle all financing and paperwork. Once the customer selects a vehicle, the representative seamlessly transitions to discussing financing options. They explain the terms and conditions, helping the customer understand their choices and select the best financing plan. The representative also manages all the necessary paperwork, ensuring that everything is completed accurately and efficiently.
- Conduct the final vehicle delivery. Finally, the representative

oversees the delivery process, making sure the vehicle is ready and that the customer is fully informed about its features and maintenance requirements. They walk the customer through any final steps, answering any last-minute questions and ensuring a smooth handover.

This single-point-of-contact approach builds trust and rapport, as customers feel understood and valued throughout the process. It eliminates the frustration of repeating information to multiple individuals and ensures a consistent and personalized experience.

This holistic approach demands a higher level of professionalism and commitment but pays off by creating a seamless and efficient process for our customers.

REAL-LIFE IMPACT

A customer named Sarah visited our dealership interested in purchasing a new SUV. Under the traditional model, she would have interacted with multiple individuals, each responsible for a different aspect of the sale. Instead, Sarah was paired with John, a cross-trained representative.

John began by discussing Sarah's needs and preferences, taking the time to understand her lifestyle and what she was looking for in a vehicle. He then showed her several SUVs that matched her criteria, providing detailed information and answering her questions. Once Sarah decided on a vehicle, John guided her through the financing options, explaining everything clearly and helping her choose the best plan. He handled all the paperwork efficiently, ensuring there were no errors or delays.

On the day of delivery, John was there to greet Sarah (either at the dealership or a destination of her preference), walk her through the vehicle's features, and ensure she felt confident with her purchase. Throughout the entire process, Sarah dealt with only one person, which made her feel valued and understood. The seamless experience left her highly satisfied, and she even left a glowing review on our website.

A COMMITMENT TO THE CUSTOMER

The one-touch experience is more than just a sales strategy; it's a commitment to putting the customer first. By minimizing the number of touchpoints and ensuring consistent, personalized service, dealerships can build stronger relationships with their customers, leading to increased satisfaction, loyalty, and profitability. I've seen firsthand the transformative power of this approach, and we continue to refine and expand it across all areas of our operations. The future of automotive sales lies in creating seamless, efficient, and customer-centric experiences, and the one-touch philosophy is at the heart of this evolution.

The one-touch experience represents a fundamental shift in how we approach customer service. It's about more than just streamlining processes; it's about placing the customer at the center of everything we do. By minimizing touchpoints and ensuring consistent, personalized service, we can build stronger relationships with our customers, leading to increased satisfaction, loyalty, and profitability. At the dealerships I co-own, we have embraced this philosophy and continue to refine and expand it across all areas of our operations. As we look to the future, the one-touch philosophy will remain a cornerstone of our commitment to delivering exceptional customer experiences and driving long-term success in the automotive industry.

You know what also drives long-term success? Inventory management.

CHAPTER 16

INVENTORY MANAGEMENT

Philosophy 13

Let's talk inventory management.

At Toyota #3, inventory management was initially a challenge due to the limited stock of only 34 new and 27 used cars. With such low inventory levels, the dealership adopted a "turn and earn" strategy, which focused on selling cars quickly to increase the allocation from the manufacturer. The goal was to move inventory rapidly to earn more vehicles to sell because the more cars sold, the more vehicles the manufacturer supplied.

To kick-start the process, the dealership had to be creative and resourceful. This involved buying cars from other stores and carefully studying market trends to identify vehicles that could be sold at a premium. The strategy required a deep understanding of customer demand and a keen eye for market opportunities to maximize profits on each sale. As the dealership began to sell more cars and generate revenue, they created the opportunity to invest more strategically in inventory management.

By gradually building up inventory and refining their approach, the dealership eventually was able to adjust their inventory strategy to better meet market demands and customer preferences. This proactive and adaptable approach allowed the store to grow from a limited inventory to a more robust and profitable operation where inventory management became a key component of their overall success.

THE FOUNDATION OF EFFECTIVE INVENTORY MANAGEMENT

In the automotive dealership world, inventory management is a crucial element that can make or break a dealership's success. Effective inventory management not only maximizes profitability but also ensures that customers have access to the vehicles they desire.

My approach to inventory management has evolved significantly over the years, driven by a focus on optimizing both new and used car inventories. By leveraging trade-ins, minimizing auction purchases, and closely tracking inventory metrics, my team and I have developed a streamlined, customer-centric inventory management system.

Effective inventory management begins with understanding the fundamental dynamics of both new and used car inventories. It's essential to keep the inventory young and in high demand to maximize floor plan assistance and minimize holding costs. For example, I remember receiving a financial statement as a sales manager and discovering an unexpected $50,000 in gross profit, which came from floor plan assistance due to having a young inventory. This highlights the importance of avoiding old-age cars and ensuring the inventory aligns with current market demands.

Managing inventory isn't only about having enough cars on the lot; it's about having the *right* cars. It's crucial to track what people are buying, how fast they are buying, and how quickly the inventory turns over. Together, my team and I ensure that we have a balance of vehicles that meet current market demands while avoiding the pitfalls of overstocking on slow-moving items.

TRACKING INVENTORY AND MARKET DEMAND

A critical aspect of effective inventory management is the ability to track market demand and inventory turnover. We utilize advanced inventory management systems like vAuto to track every aspect of our inventory and meticulously monitor what people are buying, how fast they are buying, and how quickly the inventory is turning over. This involves tracking allocations down to the series, color, and trim of each model to ensure we have the most desirable cars in stock. By doing so, we avoid the pitfall of accepting whatever the factory sends and instead order and preference cars based on market trends and seasonal demands.

For instance, during the COVID-19 pandemic, while many dealerships struggled with inventory shortages, we leveraged our knowledge of factory production and market demand to curate our inventory. By turning inventory quickly and understanding exactly what the factory was building, we grew our inventory and sold more cars, despite the challenging market conditions.

Understanding what sells quickly and what sits on the lot is crucial. By constantly analyzing sales data and market trends, we ensure that our inventory matches customer preferences.

THE IMPORTANCE OF AN INVENTORY MANAGER

Bryan's journey to becoming an inventory manager is a story of passion and dedication. For 25 years, he honed his skills on the sales floor, immersing himself in the nuances of customer preferences and market trends. He wasn't just selling cars; he was learning the pulse of the market. When the opportunity arose to manage inventory, Bryan saw it as a natural extension of his expertise. He embraced the role with enthusiasm, not just as a job but as a craft he was eager to master.

Bryan's approach to inventory management is meticulous. He analyzes sales data, anticipates demand, and ensures that the dealership is always stocked with the right mix of vehicles. His ability to focus solely on inventory allows him to excel in a way that sets him apart from others. This job is more than just a paycheck for Bryan; it's a challenge he loves to tackle every day. He thrives on the excitement of maintaining a dynamic inventory, always ready to pivot and adapt to the market's needs.

Incentivized by turnover rates, Bryan is driven to keep the inventory fresh, turning over vehicles at a pace that maximizes profits and keeps customers happy. His attention to detail and commitment to the dealership's success have made him an indispensable part of the team. Bryan's journey from a car salesman to an exceptional inventory manager shows how passion, experience, and a deep understanding of the business can lead to excellence in any role.

Managing inventory effectively is a complex task that requires dedicated resources, so someone is specifically hired to track those metrics and make informed decisions about what cars to order and when to order them.

Our full-time inventory manager's sole responsibility is to track allocations, monitor market trends, and ensure that we have the right inventory in stock. This role is critical for maintaining the right balance and ensuring that we are not overstocked with vehicles that don't sell quickly.

The inventory manager's job is to ensure that every allocation is tracked and every car's performance is monitored. This position requires a deep understanding of market trends and factory production schedules. By having someone focused solely on inventory management, we can make more informed decisions and maintain a competitive edge.

CONTINUOUS MONITORING AND ADJUSTMENTS

Inventory management is not a set-it-and-forget-it process; it requires continuous monitoring and adjustments. We track our inventory turn times daily, ensuring that cars are priced correctly and sold within a reasonable time frame. For example, if a used car has a high day supply, we either move it to a different market where it sells better or send it to auction to avoid holding costs.

We closely monitor KPIs such as gross profit per unit, inventory turnover rates, and floor plan credit utilization. These metrics help us assess the effectiveness of our inventory strategies and make necessary adjustments. For example, maintaining an inventory turnover rate of 45 days ensures that our stock remains fresh and aligned with market demand.

We had a scenario where Toyota Camrys were not moving as expected. By analyzing our data, we discovered that customers preferred different trims and colors. We adjusted our future orders accordingly, and within months, we saw a significant increase in Camry sales. This proactive approach saved us from potential losses and maximized our floor plan assistance benefits.

Additionally, we incentivize our staff to focus on selling aged inventory—our three oldest used cars and three oldest new cars come with sales incentives for the team.

This strategy not only keeps our stock fresh but also motivates our team to prioritize vehicles that might otherwise become stale.

Our service department is integrated into this process too. Service managers have a vested interest in getting used cars ready for sale quickly, understanding that faster turnaround times lead to higher customer satisfaction and profitability.

Continuous monitoring allows us to stay agile and responsive to market changes. By keeping a close eye on turn times and adjusting prices daily, we ensure that our inventory remains dynamic and aligned with customer demand.

LEVERAGING TRADE-INS FOR HIGH-QUALITY INVENTORY

By emphasizing new car sales, we generate a steady stream of high-quality trade-ins. These trade-ins typically come from loyal customers who have maintained their vehicles well, resulting in used cars in better condition with known maintenance histories. This approach contrasts sharply with the traditional reliance on auction purchases, which involve additional costs related to auction fees, transportation expenses, and unpredictable quality.

A critical aspect of leveraging trade-ins is ensuring that these vehicles are quickly assessed and reconditioned for resale. Trade-ins offer several advantages:

- Better Condition: Trade-in vehicles are often in better condition compared to auction purchases. They come with a known history and maintenance records, making them more appealing to prospective buyers.
- Cost Efficiency: Avoiding auction fees and transportation

costs associated with purchasing used cars from auctions directly impacts the bottom line. Trade-ins eliminate these additional expenses, making the process more cost-effective.

• Customer Trust: The trade-in process builds trust with customers, as they see the dealership valuing their current vehicle fairly and facilitating a seamless transition to a new car. This trust translates into higher customer satisfaction and loyalty.

Managing inventory in a dealership is a delicate balance, especially when dealing with salespeople who aren't directly impacted by inventory costs. Sales staff often prefer to keep a wide range of vehicles on hand, thinking it increases their chances of making a sale. However, slow-moving cars can clog up the lot, tying up resources and hurting profitability.

This is where a transparent and efficient inventory management process becomes crucial. At our dealership, we focus on maintaining transparency in our processes, eliminating the "man behind the curtain" approach. By sharing inventory performance data and the rationale behind inventory decisions with the sales team, we ensure everyone understands the need to move slow-moving cars.

We aim to maintain a look to book of 60%, which reflects a healthy turnover rate. This keeps the inventory dynamic and responsive to market demand, ensuring the dealership remains profitable and agile. Our clear communication and strategic approach foster a collaborative environment where everyone is on the same page, working toward the dealership's success.

And customers love our inventory so much, other dealerships in the area constantly try to buy it from us.

MINIMIZING AUCTION PURCHASES

One of the cornerstones of our inventory management philosophy is to minimize auction purchases. Auction vehicles often come with higher acquisition costs and uncertain quality, which can erode profit margins. Instead, we focus on maintaining a young inventory through trade-ins and optimizing our new car sales strategy. This helps us avoid the pitfalls associated with auctions and ensure that our used car inventory is reliable and profitable.

Minimizing auction purchases means we rely more on vehicles with a known history. This reduces the risk associated with buying used cars and ensures that we offer our customers reliable, well-maintained vehicles. Auction cars often require significant reconditioning, adding to the costs and time needed to get them ready for sale.

TRAINING AND DEVELOPMENT

Getting the staff to embrace buying fewer used cars at auction required training. First, the management team and I had to get them to accept the idea, which wasn't easy—we were met with a lot of resistance. But once we showed the sales team the numbers—that they make more money per car if they *don't* first buy it at action—the tides quickly turned.

Next, it was time to rigorously train them in inventory management practices. This included workshops on market analysis, customer demand forecasting, and effective communication with manufacturers.

Continuous learning initiatives, such as webinars and industry conferences, keep our team updated on the latest trends and best practices.

Training the team to become effective inventory managers requires a blend of discipline, attention to detail, and a willingness to learn. Some salespeople may transition to inventory management because their current work-life balance doesn't align well with the demands of sales.

I personally trained Bryan for this role. Although he had experience selling for me and understood my mindset, he still needed specific training to grasp the complexities of inventory management. Bryan was open to learning and adapted quickly, which helped him excel in his new position.

CUSTOMER FEEDBACK LOOP

Customer feedback plays a crucial role in our inventory management. We actively seek out and analyze feedback from buyers to understand their preferences and pain points. For instance, during the COVID-19 pandemic, while many dealerships struggled with inventory shortages, we used customer feedback to adjust our strategy. By leveraging insights on what the factory was producing and aligning it with customer demand, we managed to grow our inventory and maintain a steady flow of sales. This adaptability not only met customer needs but also built a reputation for reliability and responsiveness.

Enhancing customer experience through streamlined inventory management is a vital part of our dealership's success. By keeping the right cars in stock, ensuring transparency, and actively seeking customer feedback, we provide a superior buying experience that leads to higher satisfaction rates and repeat business.

CONTINUOUS INVENTORY IMPROVEMENT

A well-managed inventory fosters long-term relationships with customers. By consistently providing high-quality vehicles and transparent dealings, we build trust and loyalty. Customers who have a positive experience are more likely to return for future purchases and recommend our dealership to others. This repeat business is a testament to the effectiveness of our inventory management strategy and its impact on customer satisfaction.

It's also a testament to our focus on continuous improvement.

Continuous improvement is at the heart of our inventory management approach. We hold weekly meetings to review inventory performance, discuss market trends, and make necessary adjustments. This constant vigilance ensures that we are always ahead of the curve, ready to meet customer demands with the right vehicles at the right time. Our inventory manager plays a crucial role in these meetings, providing detailed reports on turn times, sales trends, and allocation strategies. Our proactive, data-driven approach to inventory management not only allows us to fine-tune our operations continuously, leading to a superior customer experience, but we can also meet the customers' needs and build trust and loyalty, ensuring long-term success in a competitive automotive market.

Mastering inventory management is essential for any successful dealership. By focusing on new car sales, leveraging high-quality trade-ins, and minimizing auction purchases, we have developed a robust inventory management system that drives profitability and enhances customer satisfaction. Continuous monitoring, dedicated resources, and strategic adjustments are key to maintaining an optimal inventory that meets market demands and supports long-term business success.

Convincing the team at Toyota #3 that my approach to inventory management put more money in their pockets wasn't easy, but it was worth it. This mindset and business practice not only set us apart in the competitive automotive market but also ensure that we can provide exceptional value to our customers.

The way we work with chats, PII, and AIO sets us apart too. Let's dive into Philosophy 14.

CHAPTER 17

CHATS, PII, AND AI

Philosophy 14

It was clear Toyota #3 was behind on some key innovations—specifically, there was no chat system or AI to engage customers. Chat has always been a bit of a struggle, and even though we've made improvements, it's still a challenge. Industry standards show that 18% of chat interactions convert to car sales, but we've managed to push that number to 21%. The secret? Providing information upfront. AI can engage quickly, but it's important to find a system that fits our dealership's philosophy. Chat is instantaneous, so quick and accurate responses are essential to accommodating customer needs.

Automotive dealerships are rapidly evolving, and the integration of technology has become critical. The use of chats, the management of personally identifiable information (PII), and the development of artificial intelligence (AI) and language learning models like ChapGPT are critical to enhancing customer experience and operational efficiency.

At the time of the writing of this book, our sales departments run their emails through ChatGPT first to remove trigger words to make sure the emails don't land in customers' spam boxes. We pay for everyone on our sales teams to have access to ChatGPT.

My approach has harnessed these tools to build trust, streamline operations, and drive sales while maintaining strict adherence to privacy standards.

CHATS

In today's digital age, customers expect instant responses and seamless interactions when they visit a dealership's website. The implementation of chat tools has revolutionized how we engage with potential buyers. Chats (hosted by AI) provide a platform for real-time communication, allowing customers to get immediate answers to their queries without the need for a phone call or an in-person visit.

Transparency is key when it comes to using chat tools. I believe in providing as much information as possible upfront. Together, my team and I developed a chat system designed to offer detailed information on pricing, financing options, trade-in values, and available rebates without immediately asking for personal details. This approach builds trust and ensures that customers feel informed and empowered before they decide to share their PII.

PII

Personally identifiable information (PII) refers to any data that can be used to identify a specific individual. This includes but is not limited to:

- Full name
- Address

- Email address
- Phone number
- Social Security number
- Driver's license number
- Financial information (such as credit card numbers or bank account details)
- Vehicle identification numbers (VIN)

As everyone reading this knows, PII is needed for:

- Customer identification and verification
- Processing transactions
- Credit checks and financing
- CRM
- Marketing and communication
- After-sales support and service

PII is essential for dealerships to conduct business effectively, from processing transactions and financing to managing customer relationships and providing after-sales support. However, it is equally important for dealerships to handle PII responsibly, ensuring that privacy and security measures are in place to protect customers' sensitive information. By balancing the need for PII with stringent data protection practices, dealerships can build trust and foster long-term customer relationships.

The management of PII is a critical aspect of operating a dealership in the digital age. Customers are increasingly aware of their privacy rights and expect businesses to handle their information responsibly. Our approach to PII management focuses on transparency, security, and compliance with regulatory standards.

Many dealerships make the mistake of asking for personal information too early in the conversation, which can deter potential buyers. Instead, we focus on answering questions thoroughly and promptly. This strategy encourages customers to engage more deeply with our website and, when ready, willingly provide their information. This not only improves the customer experience but also increases the likelihood of converting leads into sales.

We only ask for PII when it is absolutely necessary, and we make it clear to customers why we need their information and how it will be used. This transparency helps build trust and ensures that customers feel comfortable sharing their details with us.

Protecting customer data is a top priority. We have implemented robust security measures to safeguard PII, including encryption, secure servers, and regular audits to ensure compliance with data protection regulations.

Adhering to data protection laws such as the General Data Protection Regulation (GDPR) and regulations from the Consumer Fraud Protection Bureau (CFPB) is essential. We regularly review our data management practices to ensure compliance with these regulations and adopt industry best practices to stay ahead of potential issues.

By prioritizing security, we protect our customers and our reputation.

AI

Artificial intelligence (AI) has become an invaluable tool in managing customer interactions and streamlining sales processes. AI can handle initial inquiries, provide quick responses, and gather necessary information, allowing our human sales team to focus on more complex customer needs.

Our AI systems are programmed to manage leads efficiently. When a customer initiates a chat, the AI can answer common questions, schedule appointments, and even provide vehicle recommendations based on the customer's preferences. This not only speeds up the initial interaction but also ensures that leads are handled promptly, reducing the risk of losing potential sales.

While AI is incredibly useful, it's crucial to strike the right balance between automation and personal interaction. We ensure that our AI systems handle basic tasks, but when a conversation requires a more personal touch, a human sales representative takes over. This approach maintains the efficiency of AI while ensuring that customers feel valued and understood.

REAL-TIME ENGAGEMENT AND HIGH EXPECTATIONS

One of the most significant advantages of chat tools and AI is the ability to engage with customers in real time. For example, when a customer visits our website and starts a chat, they receive immediate responses to their queries. This instant interaction can significantly influence their decision to proceed with a purchase.

Customers using chat tools expect quick and accurate responses. To meet these expectations, we have implemented training programs for our staff to handle chat inquiries effectively and efficiently. This training includes understanding customer needs, providing clear and concise information, and knowing when to escalate the conversation to a more detailed discussion.

AI is essential for car dealerships to grow their businesses because it enhances customer service, streamlines operations, and improves decision-making. AI tools such as chatbots provide immediate, round-the-clock customer assistance, helping answer inquiries and guide users through the buying process. AI also enables personalized marketing by analyzing customer data to offer tailored recommendations.

AI-driven analytics can optimize inventory management, too,

by predicting demand trends, ensuring dealerships stock the right vehicles. This efficiency reduces costs, improves customer satisfaction, and drives sales, ultimately supporting business growth.

OVERCOMING RESISTANCE TO CHANGE

New technologies like AI and enhanced chat tools can sometimes meet resistance from staff who are accustomed to traditional methods. To address this, we involve our team in the implementation process, providing comprehensive training and highlighting the benefits of these tools in improving their workflow and enhancing customer satisfaction.

Involving staff in the implementation process is crucial for gaining their buy-in and reducing resistance. When employees feel that they are part of the decision-making process and understand the reasons behind the change, they are more likely to embrace new technologies. We start by communicating the vision and goals of the new technology, explaining how it will benefit both the dealership and the staff.

We engage our team members by seeking their feedback and suggestions during the planning phase. This collaborative approach helps in identifying potential concerns and addressing them proactively. Staff input is valuable in customizing the tools to better fit their needs and workflow, making the transition smoother.

COMPREHENSIVE TRAINING PROGRAMS

Providing comprehensive training is essential to ensure that staff are comfortable and proficient with the new technology. Our training programs are designed to be thorough and accessible, covering all aspects of the new tools and systems.

We offer hands-on training sessions where staff can interact with the new technology in a controlled environment. This practical approach helps them understand how to use the tools effectively and confidently.

After the initial training, we provide ongoing support through refresher courses, help desks, and one-on-one coaching. This continuous support helps staff address any challenges they may encounter and reinforces their skills over time.

HIGHLIGHTING THE BENEFITS

Highlighting the benefits of new technologies is crucial in overcoming resistance. We emphasize how AI and enhanced chat tools can improve workflow, increase efficiency, and enhance customer satisfaction.

AI and chat tools can handle routine inquiries and administrative tasks, freeing up staff to focus on more complex customer interactions. This leads to a more streamlined and efficient workflow, reducing stress and increasing job satisfaction.

We also demonstrate how these tools can enhance customer satisfaction by providing quicker responses, personalized interactions, and consistent service. Satisfied customers are more likely to return and recommend the dealership, benefiting everyone in the long run.

ADDRESSING CONCERNS AND MISCONCEPTIONS

Resistance often stems from concerns and misconceptions about the new technology. We address these by providing clear and transparent information. Some concerns often include:

- Job Security: One common concern is the fear of job loss due to automation. We reassure our staff that the technology is designed to assist them, not replace them. By handling repetitive tasks, AI allows staff to focus on higher-value activities that require a human touch.
- Ease of Use: Another concern is the perceived complexity of new tools. We ensure that the technology we implement is user friendly and provide step-by-step guidance to make the learning process as smooth as possible.

Sharing success stories and real-world examples of other dealerships that have successfully adopted similar technologies can be very persuasive. We highlight case studies that demonstrate tangible benefits, such as increased sales, improved customer ratings, and higher employee satisfaction.

Overcoming resistance to change when introducing new technologies like AI and enhanced chat tools requires a strategic approach. By involving the team in the implementation process, providing comprehensive training, highlighting the benefits, and addressing concerns, we can ensure a smooth transition and successful adoption. Embracing these technologies not only improves workflow and customer satisfaction but also positions the dealership for long-term success in an increasingly digital world.

STAY AHEAD OF THE CURVE

With a recent iOS update, around 40% of people who read emails via the iPhone Mail app experienced a new feature where the app categorizes emails based on specific keywords using AI. This means emails can be automatically sorted into categories like promotions, purchases, or other relevant sections, improving the user's inbox management experience.

For businesses, especially in industries that rely on lead generation, such as car dealerships, lead response strategies can leverage this AI-driven categorization by including keywords in their communications that ensure emails are correctly sorted and not lost in less relevant folders. Including specific terms like "appointment," "quote," or "urgent" in the subject line or email body may help the AI categorize the email in a way that keeps it visible to the customer, enhancing response rates and improving communication efficiency. This targeted use of keywords could ensure that vital customer interactions remain prioritized.

By understanding how AI categorizes email content, businesses can optimize their lead response, ensuring key information is captured by both AI systems and human readers and emails stay relevant in the recipient's inbox.

The integration of chats, AI, and PII management in our dealership has transformed how we interact with customers and handle their information. By prioritizing transparency, leveraging advanced technology, and maintaining strict data protection standards, we have created a more efficient, customer-centric sales process.

As the automotive industry continues to evolve, our commitment to embracing these tools ensures that we stay ahead of the curve, delivering exceptional service and building lasting relationships with our customers.

This commitment to embracing new tools and maintaining high standards ensures that we stay ahead of the curve, delivering exceptional service and building lasting relationships with our customers. As the automotive industry continues to evolve, our proactive approach positions us for sustained success and leadership in the market.

Chats, PII management, and AI have significantly transformed our dealership's operations.

CHAPTER 18

THE SERVICE BDC

Philosophy 15

At both Toyota #2 and #3, our service BDC operates as the central hub for communication between the dealership and our service customers. Unlike traditional service departments, where customers often experience fragmented interactions and miscommunication, our service BDC staff are equipped with all the information they need upfront to provide a seamless and transparent customer experience.

Previously, the service process followed the traditional, fragmented model that most dealerships still use. In that system, customers had to interact with several different people—first speaking with a BDC representative to schedule an appointment, then a service advisor at the dealership, and, finally, the technician who worked on their vehicle. This approach often led to confusion, miscommunication, and inefficiencies, making the process frustrating for both customers and staff.

The biggest challenge in the traditional service BDC model is that it acts as a middleman, relaying messages and information between the customer and the service department without direct knowledge of the technical side. This often leads to delays, inaccurate estimates, and a disconnect between what the customer expects and what actually happens during their service visit.

One of the reasons is that the traditional service BDC model is fragmented. The customer has to repeat their concerns to multiple people, often leading to miscommunication. For example, if the BDC doesn't fully capture the issue, it may cause delays when the customer arrives because the service advisor needs to ask more questions. These inefficiencies not only extend the time customers spend waiting for service but also erode their confidence in the process. And the back-and-forth between departments can result in inconsistent communication about service updates, costs, and timelines, leaving the customer feeling out of the loop.

Customer satisfaction and retention have increased because of this new service BDC philosophy. By removing the inefficiencies of the *traditional* service BDC model, we have reduced wait times, improved communication, and created a more personalized experience that leaves our customers feeling confident in their choice to return to us for all their vehicle needs. It has allowed us to offer a level of service that goes beyond what most dealerships provide, building trust and delivering value at every interaction.

TRANSPARENCY AND CUSTOMER TRUST

The service BDC model is about more than just streamlining operations—it's built on the foundations of transparency and trust, essential values for long-term customer relationships. By giving each customer all the information upfront, we eliminate the back-and-forth between different staff members, reducing confusion and ensuring a smoother experience.

When customers schedule a service, our BDC staff provide

them with detailed, itemized quotes before any work begins. By pulling up each vehicle's service history and MPI records, our service BDC can identify any other services that may be due or were previously deferred. This includes a breakdown of labor costs and parts pricing and an estimated timeline for completion. The goal is to ensure that there are no surprises when it comes time to pay. It's about managing expectations upfront. Because of our complete transparency in every interaction, customers feel more confident in our recommendations, knowing that we have their best interests in mind.

This proactive approach also shows our customers that we're attentive to their vehicles' needs, helping them maintain those vehicles in peak condition. It saves them the hassle of multiple visits, too, allowing us to address all necessary repairs and maintenance in one go. This way, we improve the efficiency of our shop operations but also demonstrate a level of thoroughness that customers appreciate.

A great example of this is when a customer calls about a tire replacement. Rather than just scheduling the tire service, our service BDC reviews the vehicle's records and notices that brake pads were nearing the end of their lifespan during the last inspection. The customer is informed and given the option to address the brake issue during the same appointment, streamlining the process and ensuring the car leaves the shop fully serviced. It's about being proactive, which strengthens the customer's trust in us.

This commitment to transparency also extends to how we manage our shop capacity. With advanced scheduling tools, we optimize appointment times and ensure service bays are used efficiently. Our service BDC staff set realistic expectations for appointment durations and availability, avoiding overbooking and minimizing customer wait times. By respecting the customer's time and being upfront about how long service will take, we demonstrate a level of respect that translates into higher satisfaction and loyalty.

Ultimately, this service BDC model is about creating an environment where customers feel cared for and valued. It's not just about fixing cars; it's about creating a seamless experience where trust, transparency, and efficiency drive the relationship forward. And by building that trust, we're not just enhancing the customer experience; we're also driving long-term business growth, with higher customer retention and greater overall satisfaction.

COMPREHENSIVE TRAINING AND EMPOWERMENT

We knew that adopting a transparent service BDC would only be as effective as the people behind it. Transitioning to this new system required more than just logistical changes; it called for a comprehensive approach to training. Ensuring that our team understood the new process, embraced the philosophy, and felt confident in their expanded roles was *crucial* to making the new service BDC model work seamlessly for our customers.

Training and empowering our service BDC staff is critical for maintaining high standards of service. All team members, including non-technicians, are well versed in our processes and equipped to handle a wide range of inquiries. Our training programs cover everything from basic customer service skills to advanced diagnostic techniques. This ensures that all service BDC staff can provide detailed, accurate information and set the right expectations for customers. Continuous learning is encouraged through workshops, seminars, and online courses, keeping our team updated on the latest industry trends and technologies.

Empowering service BDC staff to make informed decisions without constant supervision improves efficiency and customer satisfaction. They are authorized to quote parts, provide service estimates, and make scheduling decisions, ensuring that customers receive immediate, comprehensive answers to their questions.

THE NEW-SCHOOL MODEL OF TRANSPARENCY AND TRUST

The service BDC has become a vital component of our dealership's success, not just driving efficiency but also deepening the relationships we build with our customers. When I first took over the store, the service department mirrored the traditional fragmented model that many dealerships still follow. Multiple points of contact, miscommunications, and inefficiencies led to frustrated customers and missed opportunities. Today, we've redefined that approach entirely by integrating a one-touch philosophy into our service BDC, streamlining communication and ensuring each customer feels truly taken care of.

By leveraging the expertise of our service team and providing extensive training, we've transformed the way we operate. At Toyota #3, every interaction is rooted in transparency, and our customers appreciate that consistency. From the moment they contact us to the time they drive away, they experience a seamless, straightforward process that fosters trust. This isn't just about making things easier. It's about showing customers that we respect their time, value their loyalty, and care about their experience at every step.

The evolution didn't happen overnight. It took dedication, a commitment to customer satisfaction, and a willingness to break from traditional methods that weren't serving us. By making the service BDC experience transparent for our customers, we've seen higher retention rates, improved customer satisfaction, and a service department that's more efficient than ever. This transformation is a testament to what's possible when we focus on building long-term relationships with customers, putting customers' needs first, and adapting to industry changes.

The store's journey from an old-school model to one driven by transparency and trust isn't just a success story for our dealership; it's a model for how the industry can evolve. As we continue to refine our processes and maintain this commitment to excellence, we ensure that the store remains at the forefront, delivering the exceptional service our customers deserve while securing our place as an industry leader for years to come.

With all that said, it's time to dive into fixed ops, the next philosophy.

CHAPTER 19

THIS IS HOW WE DO FIXED OPS

Philosophy 16

Traditionally, fixed operations (fixed ops) departments in automotive dealerships were managed with a focus on maintaining distinct and often siloed roles for service advisors, technicians, and parts departments. In many dealerships, these departments operated independently, with little crossover or collaboration, which often resulted in inefficiencies and missed opportunities to provide seamless customer experiences. This fragmented approach, while functional, often left customers feeling like they were constantly passed from one department to another, especially when it came to managing appointments, diagnosing vehicle issues, and communicating service updates.

At Toyota #3, we knew there was a better way to approach fixed ops. Rather than maintaining a disconnected, traditional system, we focused on streamlining our operations to create a more cohesive and transparent process. We embraced a customer-centric philosophy that emphasized transparency and clear communication at every stage of the service journey. The goal was to enhance the customer experience by breaking down traditional silos and leveraging technology to keep customers informed, reduce wait times, and improve service quality.

Fixed ops are essential for maintaining customer satisfaction and loyalty. My approach to managing fixed ops has been shaped by years of experience, focusing on efficiency, transparency, and technology to enhance the customer experience. I'm going to share the strategies and practices we've implemented to ensure our fixed ops department not only meets but exceeds customer expectations.

Fixed ops are critical to the long-term success of a dealership. They provide a steady revenue stream and foster customer loyalty through consistent, high-quality service. A well-managed fixed ops department can turn a one-time buyer into a lifelong customer.

EFFICIENT SERVICE

Efficiency in the service department is crucial for minimizing customer wait times and maximizing shop productivity. We achieve this through meticulous scheduling and workflow management.

We use advanced scheduling tools to allocate time slots and ensure that each service bay is utilized effectively. Planning ahead and setting clear expectations with customers allows us to avoid overbooking and ensures that each job is completed on time.

We also use state-of-the-art tools for diagnostics to enable our technicians to quickly identify and address issues, reducing the time vehicles spend in the shop. These tools ensure accuracy in repairs, leading to higher customer satisfaction and fewer repeat visits for the same issue.

UPFRONT PRICING AND INFORMED RECOMMENDATIONS

Our service processes are transparent from start to finish. We provide customers with detailed, itemized quotes before they ever step into a dealership and before any work begins. This includes an explanation of each service, the cost, and the time required. By eliminating surprises, we build trust and ensure that customers feel confident in the value they receive.

We maintain comprehensive service records for each vehicle, which allows us to provide informed recommendations based on the vehicle's history. This transparency helps customers make better decisions about their vehicle maintenance and repairs.

CLEAR COMMUNICATION

A new customer had a flat tire and had reached out to her previous dealership, looking for assistance. All she needed was a straightforward answer: how much would it cost to repair or replace her tire? Unfortunately, the person who answered the phone didn't have access to the service pricing and couldn't help her. They transferred her to the service manager, but after multiple attempts and calls, she didn't get an answer. Frustrated and left without guidance, she eventually turned to a tire shop to get the issue resolved. This experience showed her the importance of clear communication and is one of the reasons she's now our customer. At our dealership, she knows that if she has a question, she'll always get a prompt, informed response.

Effective communication is crucial in the service department because it ensures that customers are well informed and confident in the services they receive. Here's a deeper look into how we implement clear communication at every stage of the service process.

WARM WELCOME AND ACTIVE LISTENING

The communication process begins the moment a customer contacts our dealership. Whether they reach out via phone or email or visit in person, our service advisors (or client advisors) greet them warmly and actively listen to their concerns. This initial interaction sets the tone for the entire service experience, making customers feel valued and understood.

ACCURATE DOCUMENTATION

Accurately documenting the customer's concerns is essential. Our advisors use detailed intake forms and digital tools to capture every detail of the issue. This documentation ensures that no information is lost or misunderstood, providing a solid foundation for the service process.

DETAILED EXPLANATIONS AND SERVICE REPORTS

When it comes to recommending services, clarity is key. Our advisors take the time to explain the issues identified, the recommended repairs or maintenance, and the reasons behind these recommendations. They use plain language, avoiding technical jargon that might confuse the customer. For instance, instead of saying, "You need new brake pads," they might say, "Your brake pads are worn down to a point where they can no longer provide effective braking, which could compromise your safety. This is the cost of new brake pads."

Customers also receive a detailed report of the services performed, including any future maintenance recommendations. This report helps them understand what was done, why it was necessary, and what to look out for in the future. It's a valuable tool for maintaining their vehicle's health and ensuring they return for regular maintenance.

VISUAL AIDS

To enhance understanding, we often use visual aids. This could include showing the customer the worn parts or using diagrams to explain how a particular system works. Visual aids make complex information more accessible and help customers grasp the importance of the recommended services.

REGULAR UPDATES

Keeping customers informed throughout the service process is crucial. We provide regular updates on the status of their vehicle, whether it's through phone calls, text messages, or emails. These updates might include estimated completion times, any unexpected findings, and progress reports. Regular communication ensures that customers are never left in the dark so they can can plan their day accordingly.

If there are any delays or additional issues discovered during the service, we communicate these transparently. Our advisors explain the reasons for the delays, the impact on the overall timeline, and any additional costs involved. This honesty helps build trust, even when the news isn't what the customer was hoping for.

CLEAR BILLING

Once the service is completed, clear billing is another aspect of effective communication. We provide itemized invoices that break down the costs of parts, labor, and any additional services. Advisors go over the bill with the customer, answering any questions and ensuring there are no surprises.

CUSTOMER FEEDBACK

Continuous improvement is essential for maintaining high standards in fixed ops. We regularly review our processes and seek feedback from both customers and staff to identify areas for improvement.

After the service, we follow up with customers to gather feedback on their experience. This might be through a survey, a phone call, or an email. We ask specific questions about the clarity of communication, the quality of service, and their overall satisfaction. This feedback helps us continually improve our processes and ensures that we meet our customers' needs. By addressing these areas, we continuously enhance the quality of our service.

STAFF TRAINING AND DEVELOPMENT

Service staff training and development are essential for delivering exceptional service and maintaining a competitive edge. By ensuring our staff are up to date with the latest industry practices and technologies, we foster continuous improvement and high performance. This includes both technical training for technicians and customer service training for advisors, ensuring all team members are well equipped to meet and exceed customer expectations.

TECHNICAL TRAINING FOR TECHNICIANS

Regular training keeps technicians at the forefront of industry advancements, covering new vehicle technologies, manufacturer-specific procedures, and advanced diagnostics. This ensures quick, accurate diagnoses and effective repairs.

We support technicians in obtaining industry certifications like ASE and offer continuous education opportunities to refine their skills and stay updated on advancements.

INTEGRATED TRAINING PROGRAMS

Joint workshops and role-playing exercises foster teamwork between technicians and advisors, enhancing mutual understanding and cooperation. Practical workshops allow technicians to apply their knowledge on real vehicles, mastering complex repair techniques and staying proficient with new tools.

Leadership programs develop future supervisors and strategic thinkers, helping staff understand their roles in the dealership's success.

We continuously adapt our training programs to address new challenges, such as introducing modules on electric vehicle maintenance in response to growing demand.

CUSTOMER SERVICE TRAINING FOR ADVISORS

Customer service training focuses on effective communication, service recommendations, and conflict resolution, ensuring advisors build strong relationships with customers.

Advisors receive training on vehicle features, maintenance services, and the benefits of each, enabling them to provide informed recommendations.

Training on CRM systems and digital tools ensures advisors can manage customer interactions efficiently, providing timely updates and maintaining accurate records.

Investing in staff training and development ensures high standards of service and competitiveness. Comprehensive technical and customer service training, integrated programs, and continuous feedback foster a culture of collaboration and excellence. Our commitment to supporting staff and exceeding customer expectations drives our ongoing success.

EXCELLENCE IN FIXED OPS

Fixed operations are a vital component of any successful dealership. By focusing on providing clear communication and efficient service, leveraging technology, and maintaining transparency, we have created a fixed ops department that not only meets but exceeds customer expectations. Continuous improvement and a customer-centric approach ensure that we build long-lasting relationships with our customers, driving long-term success for our dealership.

Clear communication ensures customers are well informed about every aspect of their service experience, building trust and confidence. Efficiency in our service operations minimizes wait times and ensures timely repairs, enhancing customer satisfaction and operational productivity. Leveraging technology, we use advanced diagnostic tools and automated communication systems to improve service delivery and operational efficiency. Transparency through upfront pricing, detailed service reports, and video multipoint inspections (MPIs) builds trust and reassures customers of high-quality service. Continuous improvement keeps our fixed ops department competitive and responsive to changing customer needs, driven by regular training and feedback.

Our customer-centric approach prioritizes customer needs and preferences, creating personalized service experiences that build long-lasting relationships and drive repeat business. The integration of these elements ensures our fixed ops department exceeds customer expectations, driving long-term success for our dealership through trust, strong relationships, and consistent high-quality service.

Through strategic focus on key areas, we have created a service environment that delights customers and enhances loyalty. As we continue to refine and improve our processes, our commitment to excellence in fixed operations will ensure that we remain a leader in the automotive service industry, providing exceptional value and satisfaction to our customers.

Now, let's dive a little deeper into the nuances of fixed ops, starting with flat rates versus salaries and hourly pay.

CHAPTER 20

FLAT RATES VERSUS SALARY OR HOURLY PAY

Philosophy 17

The service department at Toyota #2 was entirely based on a flat-rate pay system for technicians. The way this system works is that technicians are paid based on the number of hours billed for a job, regardless of the actual time it takes to complete it. While this can be a motivator for efficiency, it often leads to technicians cutting corners to maximize their pay, which compromises the quality of service.

Operating entirely on a flat-rate payment system caused a lot of problems. Flat-rate pushes technicians to work faster in order to make more money, but that often means sacrificing quality and attention to detail. At Toyota #2, that meant the environment was high stress, with techs feeling like they had to rush through jobs just to keep up. There was no system in place to make sure the work was done efficiently or correctly, and it showed.

At Toyota #2, this flat-rate system wasn't benefiting the department or its employees. Many technicians were stressed, rushed, and not producing quality work. Over time, HR and I noticed the department's performance and morale were suffering as a result. There was a lack of management oversight on how technicians were performing their jobs, leading to inefficiencies and lower customer satisfaction.

We knew something had to change, so we decided to move the department to a combination of salary-based pay with flat-rate incentives. Our goal was to take some of the pressure off the techs by giving them a stable base salary while still letting them earn more if they worked efficiently.

THE FLAWS OF THE FLAT-RATE SYSTEM

Some of what you are going to read in this chapter is a bit repetitive, and that's intentional because the debate between flat-rate, hourly, and salary compensation models for technicians is ongoing. Each model has its advantages and drawbacks, affecting not only the technicians' livelihoods but also the overall efficiency and morale within the service department. My approach to compensation has been shaped by years of experience, focusing on fairness, productivity, and long-term sustainability. This chapter outlines the rationale behind moving away from flat-rate and embracing hourly and salary pay structures for a dealership's fixed ops team.

The flat-rate system, where technicians are paid based on the number of hours they bill regardless of the actual time worked, is prevalent in many dealerships. But this system has significant drawbacks that can negatively impact both the quality of work and technician morale.

PROMOTING BAD HABITS

Flat-rate often incentivizes technicians to cut corners to maximize billable hours, leading to subpar work quality. For example, a technician might rush through a job to move on to the next, increasing their earnings at the expense of thoroughness and customer satisfaction. This not only jeopardizes the integrity of the repairs but also undermines the dealership's reputation for quality service.

STRESS AND UNCERTAINTY

Technicians working under a flat-rate system face considerable stress and uncertainty regarding their income. They begin the week without knowing how much they will earn, which can lead to financial instability and job dissatisfaction. This uncertainty can cause high turnover rates as technicians seek more stable employment elsewhere.

MANAGEMENT CHALLENGES

In a flat-rate system, managers often focus on numbers, neglecting to help technicians improve their efficiency or quality of work. They don't emphasize optimizing shop capacity or scheduling to ensure steady workflow. However, we now have a service manager who understands how to balance everything. Having been a skilled technician, he actively trains others to be more efficient, which reduces stress and increases job satisfaction. If issues persist, our progressive discipline policy ensures they're addressed. This hands-on management style fosters a more supportive and productive work environment.

The flat-rate system is often a sign of weak management. It places the burden of productivity entirely on the technicians, absolving managers of their responsibility to ensure jobs are done efficiently and correctly. Instead of mentoring and developing their teams, managers might rely on the flat-rate system to self-regulate productivity.

TRANSITIONING TO HOURLY AND SALARY MODELS

Recognizing the flaws in our compensation structure, we made the decision to transition to hourly and salary-based models. However, this shift wasn't without its challenges, particularly when it came to management buy-in. Over the course of five years, we went through four different service managers, all of whom struggled to adapt to the new system. They were accustomed to focusing solely on the numbers, without engaging with the technicians or working to improve shop efficiency.

The turning point came when we hired our fifth service manager—a former technician himself. He understood the techs' perspective and recognized the importance of mentoring them and properly organizing job dispatch. His leadership transformed the department. Morale improved, and productivity surged. Our service department became one of the most profitable in the organization.

Once management was on board, the technicians embraced the change, and it became clear that this was the right direction for our team.

The shift from flat-rate to hourly and salary models required careful planning and a change in management philosophy, but the results have been overwhelmingly positive and beneficial.

FAIR COMPENSATION

Hourly and salary pay structures provide technicians with stable, predictable income, reducing stress and financial uncertainty. Technicians are paid fairly for their time and expertise (pay ranges based on time of employment and level of certifications), regardless of the job's complexity or duration. This stability fosters a more positive work environment and encourages long-term career development.

When transitioning from a flat-rate pay system to a more balanced compensation structure for technicians, it's important to consider those who thrived on flat-rate. One approach is to set the base pay at 75–80% of their previous earnings while adding a flat-rate incentive for hours produced. This hybrid model ensures fair compensation while reducing stress, as technicians still benefit from high-earning months without the pressure of cutting corners. Maintaining a higher base salary discourages reverting to bad habits common in strict flat-rate systems.

EMPHASIZING QUALITY

With hourly and salary models, technicians can focus on the quality of their work without the pressure to rush. This leads to better repairs and higher customer satisfaction. For example, a technician can take the necessary time to diagnose and fix an issue correctly the first time rather than resorting to quick fixes that might result in repeat visits.

The time it takes to complete a job needs to be monitored by the management or dispatcher. If a tech is doing the job too slowly, that can be addressed in a coaching session.

IMPROVED TECHNICIAN RETENTION

Since implementing the new pay structures, we have seen a significant increase in technician retention. Technicians appreciate the stability and fairness of their compensation, and this has led to a full, stable workforce. For instance, at Toyota #2, we doubled the number of technicians from seven to fourteen, and our shop is now at full capacity. We also have a waiting list of techs who want to work with us.

INCREASED PRODUCTIVITY AND MORALE

Our highest-producing technician is now on a salary. His stress levels have dropped, and he no longer feels pressure to compete for high-paying jobs. This technician now also takes on a mentoring role, helping to train newer technicians and promote a positive work environment.

ENHANCED TRAINING AND DEVELOPMENT

When our former service manager was replaced, it was a game changer. The previous manager had been in the industry for years, and while they were smart, they were stuck in their ways. They resisted every improvement I tried to introduce, believing technicians should naturally want to work faster for more pay. For two years, we lost $30,000 to $40,000 a month because there was no real leadership. The mindset was reactive, with no coaching or involvement in daily operations.

Finally, HR and I brought in a new service manager who believes in our process. Instead of sitting back, this manager is out on the floor with the technicians every day, ensuring efficiency, paying attention to job dispatch, and coaching the team. It isn't just about end-of-month numbers; it's about monitoring and managing every step of the way.

With the new manager in place, we went from losing $30,000 a month to making $70,000 to $90,000 in profits each month. That's over a million dollars a year, all thanks to a shift in mindset. I couldn't believe it. Two years of resistance cost me nearly $2.4 million, and all it took was someone who truly understood the value of hard work and hands-on management.

Managers play a more active role in training and developing their teams under the hourly and salary models. They are responsible for ensuring technicians are efficient and skilled, which involves continuous education and mentorship. This approach not only improves job performance but also builds a culture of excellence and collaboration.

HIGH PRODUCTIVITY LEVELS

While transitioning away from flat-rate at Toyota #2, we encountered a common objection: that hourly and salary pay structures reduce productivity. The transition was met also with resistance from the service manager, who preferred the old system.

By setting clear expectations and providing ongoing training, though, we have maintained high productivity levels. Technicians are motivated by a supportive work environment and opportunities for professional growth rather than the pressure to bill hours.

Change management was critical in this transition. We ensured that our service managers were fully on board and understood the benefits of the new system. Having regular meetings, providing transparent communication, and addressing concerns directly were key.

The debate between flat-rate, hourly, and salary compensation models is more than a matter of preference; it reflects broader values of fairness, quality, and management effectiveness. By moving away from the flat-rate system, we have created a more stable, productive, and satisfied workforce. This transition not only improves the quality of service we provide to our customers but also ensures the long-term success and sustainability of our dealership. Embracing hourly and salary pay structures aligns with our commitment to excellence and positions us as a leader in the automotive service industry.

Embracing video technology is another of my philosophies. Keep reading to learn why.

CHAPTER 21

VIDEO MPIS

Philosophy 18

Utilizing video for our MPIs (multipoint inspections) wasn't practiced at Toyota #3 at first. It wasn't something I initially brought in, but it quickly became a priority. A lot of manufacturers make video MPIs mandatory, and for good reason. They're essential to the transparency of the process.

Video MPI isn't something new or revolutionary. It's something that should have been standard practice for a decade. It's crucial to show the customer exactly what's going on with their vehicle, so they can trust the recommendations we're making. The video not only makes things clearer for the customer, but it also ensures that our technicians are more thorough and accountable. It's now a key part of our service process and is used consistently to provide a higher level of service and transparency for our customers.

THE IMPORTANCE OF VIDEO MPIS

In the modern automotive service landscape, transparency and trust are paramount. One of the most effective tools we have implemented to enhance these values is the video multipoint inspection (MPI). This approach allows customers to see exactly what our technicians see, providing a clear and honest assessment of their vehicle's condition. By prioritizing transparency and leveraging technology, we have transformed our service operations and significantly improved customer satisfaction.

Video MPIs are not just a technological upgrade; they are a fundamental shift in how we communicate with our customers. Traditional paper MPIs are often met with skepticism, as customers have no way to verify the findings themselves. Video MPIs, on the other hand, provide a visual confirmation of the technician's assessment, building trust and credibility.

ENHANCING TRANSPARENCY

By showing customers the exact issues with their vehicles through video, we eliminate any doubts or misunderstandings. For instance, a customer can see the wear on their brake pads or the condition of their tires, making it easier for them to understand the necessity of recommended services. This transparency leads to higher acceptance rates for repairs and maintenance, as customers feel more informed and confident in their decisions.

BUILDING TRUST

Trust is a critical component of customer loyalty. When customers see our technicians explaining and demonstrating the issues in real time, it reinforces their trust in our dealership. They appreciate the honesty and feel reassured that we are not recommending unnecessary services. This trust translates into repeat business and positive word-of-mouth referrals.

IMPLEMENTING VIDEO MPIS

Introducing video MPIs required a strategic approach to ensure smooth adoption by both staff and customers. Here's how we implemented this system effectively.

PROVIDING THE RIGHT TOOLS

We equipped our technicians with the necessary tools to record high-quality videos. This included providing iPads and other recording devices that are easy to use and capable of capturing clear, detailed footage. By investing in the right technology, we ensured that our technicians could perform their jobs efficiently and effectively.

TRAINING AND EMPOWERING TECHNICIANS

Not all technicians are comfortable being on camera, so it was essential to provide thorough training and support. We emphasized that the videos are for the customers' benefit and that technicians do not need to be on camera themselves. Instead, the focus is on the vehicle and the work being done.

OVERCOMING INITIAL RESISTANCE

To encourage adoption, we made it clear that video MPIs are mandatory in our stores. Technicians understood that this was nonnegotiable, and we supported them through the transition with continuous training and positive reinforcement. By highlighting the benefits and showing successful examples, we helped technicians become more comfortable and proficient with the new process.

INCENTIVIZING PARTICIPATION

To further motivate our technicians, we implemented incentive programs based on the quality and effectiveness of their videos.

PERFORMANCE-BASED REWARDS

Technicians who consistently produce high-quality videos and achieve high customer engagement rates are rewarded. This includes bonuses for high production hours and recognition for the most-viewed videos. These incentives not only encourage compliance but also promote a culture of excellence and continuous improvement.

CONTINUOUS FEEDBACK AND IMPROVEMENT

We regularly review the videos produced by our technicians, providing constructive feedback and celebrating successes. Managers watch every video before it is sent to the customer, ensuring quality control and providing immediate guidance if improvements are needed. This continuous feedback loop helps maintain high standards and encourages technicians to take pride in their work.

POSITIVE FEEDBACK AND TRUST

The response from customers has been overwhelmingly positive. They appreciate the transparency and feel more involved in the maintenance of their vehicles.

Customers now expect video MPIs as part of their service experience. If a video is not provided, even if the vehicle is in good condition, they often inquire about it. This expectation underscores the importance of maintaining consistency in our service delivery.

The transparency provided by video MPIs has led to numerous positive reviews and increased trust in our dealership. Customers feel more confident in their service decisions and are more likely to return for future maintenance and repairs.

A memorable example of the impact of video MPIs involves a customer who was initially skeptical about the recommended brake replacement. After receiving a video showing the worn brake pads and a clear explanation from the technician, the customer appreciated the transparency and approved the service. This interaction resulted in not only a completed sale but also a loyal customer who has returned multiple times for other services.

Video MPIs have revolutionized our service operations by enhancing transparency, building trust, and improving customer satisfaction. By providing clear visual evidence of vehicle issues, we have empowered our customers to make informed decisions and reinforced their trust in our dealership. The successful implementation of video MPIs demonstrates our commitment to innovation and excellence in customer service. As we continue to refine this approach, we remain dedicated to providing an exceptional service experience that keeps our customers coming back.

CHAPTER 22

COMBINE YOUR SALES AND SERVICE ADVISORS

Philosophy 19

At about every other dealership in the US, sales and service advisors are different people. It's a standard that has always been in place but one I hope to change.

In the automotive service industry, the traditional separation of sales and service advisors often leads to communication breakdowns and inefficiencies. My approach challenges this conventional model by proposing a unified role where a single individual handles both customer interactions and vehicle repairs.

Traditionally, sales and service advisors have distinct responsibilities.

Sales advisors and service advisors serve distinct roles in a dealership, each focusing on a different stage of the customer's relationship with the dealership. Sales advisors, also known as client advisors, guide customers through the process of purchasing a new or used vehicle. They help customers identify their needs, recommend suitable vehicles, and manage the financial aspects of the purchase. Their goal is to ensure that the customer feels confident in their decision and to close the sale, often building initial customer relationships that may lead to future transactions like trade-ins or upgrades.

Service advisors, on the other hand, handle the post-purchase phase of vehicle ownership. Their primary responsibility is to act as the bridge between the customer and the service department, ensuring the customer's vehicle receives the necessary maintenance and repairs. Service advisors listen to customer concerns, coordinate with technicians, and provide updates about the progress and cost of repairs. Their role is critical in maintaining customer loyalty through ongoing care, as they help extend the life of the vehicle and ensure customer satisfaction.

The main difference between the two roles lies in their focus: sales advisors are dedicated to the transaction of buying a vehicle, while service advisors manage the vehicle's ongoing maintenance. Sales advisors handle the early stages of the customer's dealership experience, while service advisors maintain the long-term relationship through regular vehicle care and maintenance.

We're in the early stages of combining the sales and service advisor roles into one: the client advisor. We're exploring a new approach where the person who originally sold you the car will also take care of all your service needs.

This change is aimed at enhancing the one-touch experience we've been working toward. By having the same person handle both sales and service, we can build stronger, more trusting relationships with our customers. It ensures continuity throughout the entire life cycle of the vehicle, with one person taking ownership of both the sale and the service experience.

That said, we're still working out the kinks, testing this integration to see how it impacts both our operations and customer satisfaction. It's a learning curve, and while the long-term vision is clear, there are still adjustments and refinements to be made.

I've learned that combining the sales and service advisor roles requires buy-in from everyone. It's not just about getting employees, service managers, and sales managers excited. It involves coordinating across multiple departments and ensuring each one is aligned. Technicians are impacted. The BDC and dispatch teams are impacted. Most importantly, the customer experience is impacted. Even something as fundamental as ordering parts affects the entire operation. Every department plays a role, and it's crucial to bring them together for a seamless, efficient process. With transparency and trust at the core of this initiative, we're optimistic about the potential this has to further elevate our customer service.

THE BENEFITS OF A UNIFIED ROLE

Combining the roles of sales and service advisors ensures that customers interact with the same person throughout their entire service experience, from initial contact to the completion of repairs.

One of the biggest advantages of transitioning to a more streamlined service process is the consistency it creates in customer relationships. Imagine having the same person who not only understands your specific needs but knows your vehicle inside and out. This kind of personal connection builds trust, and when customers trust the person working on their car, it deepens their satisfaction and loyalty. It's more than just a transactional relationship. Customers feel like they're being taken care of by someone who genuinely knows them and their vehicle history, which makes a world of difference. It turns a routine service visit into an experience that keeps them coming back.

On top of that, efficiency takes a huge leap forward, and the workflow becomes much smoother. Customers no longer have to wait while messages are relayed between different people. They get quicker updates, faster service, and an overall better experience. It's a win-win situation: customers appreciate the faster, more personalized service, and the team benefits from a more streamlined, productive environment. Everyone leaves happy, and the dealership's reputation for quality service continues to grow.

A WORTHWHILE INVESTMENT

One of the major challenges we continue to face at Toyota #3 is the constant breakdown in communication between sales and service advisors. Every time information passes from one person to another, there's a risk of miscommunication—whether it's a misunderstanding about the vehicle's issues or confusion over what repairs are needed. This creates a frustrating experience for customers, who often feel out of the loop and disconnected from what's happening with their vehicle. They call in for updates, only to be met with vague answers or the need to wait while someone checks with a technician. This lack of clear communication leaves them feeling uneasy and uncertain about the process.

This also delays repairs and impacts overall productivity.

It's clear that this fragmented process isn't just a frustration for our team—it's eroding customer trust and creating bottlenecks in the workflow.

Combining the roles of sales and service advisors into a single client advisor position will offer numerous benefits, including improved communication, enhanced customer trust, and increased operational efficiency.

This innovative model will position us at the forefront of the future of the automotive service industry and set new standards for excellence and customer satisfaction.

CHAPTER 23

THE FUTURE OF AUTOMOTIVE

Whether you like it or not, Tesla is reshaping the automotive industry...and it's succeeding. The direct-to-consumer model is gaining significant traction and setting a new standard for car sales. By eliminating traditional dealership middlemen, Tesla offers a streamlined buying experience that appeals to modern consumers.

Buyers can order vehicles directly from Tesla's website, customizing their features and specifications, and have them delivered directly to their homes. This direct approach allows Tesla to maintain control over the entire sales process, providing a seamless and transparent experience. The ability to bypass the often lengthy and complex negotiations associated with traditional dealerships has been a key factor in the model's growing popularity.

Despite some criticisms about the reliability and build quality of Tesla vehicles, the brand's focus on consumer convenience and direct interaction has proven highly successful. In 2023, Tesla dominated the EV sector, accounting for 55% of all EV sales in the US. The Tesla Model Y, in particular, stood out as the bestselling electric vehicle, with 394,497 units sold. The Model 3 followed closely behind with 220,910 units sold. Together, these two models secured the top two spots in EV sales in the US for 2023.[19]

Tesla's approach aligns with the expectations of contemporary buyers who prioritize efficiency, speed, and control in their purchasing decisions. The company's user-friendly website and mobile app allow consumers to manage every aspect of their purchase, from financing to delivery, at their convenience. This consumer-centric strategy not only enhances the purchasing experience but also reinforces customer trust and satisfaction, contributing to Tesla's strong market presence and brand loyalty.

Tesla's commitment to service convenience further enhances its direct-to-consumer model. The company offers a range of convenient service options, including mobile service units that travel to customers' locations to perform repairs and maintenance. This eliminates the need for customers to visit service centers, saving them time and effort.

The focus on delivering high-quality service at the customer's convenience has significantly boosted satisfaction and loyalty, as customers appreciate the hassle-free maintenance experience. One key factor is the company's emphasis on convenience, such as over-the-air (OTA) updates, which allow customers to receive software upgrades and fixes without visiting a service center. This hassle-free experience ensures that vehicles stay up to date and optimized, with minimal disruption to the customer.

Additionally, Tesla's mobile service offering allows technicians to perform repairs and maintenance at the customer's home or workplace. This approach greatly enhances convenience, eliminating the need for customers to visit a dealership, which is traditionally a pain point in the automotive industry. Customers appreciate the personalized, seamless experience, contributing to Tesla's high Net Promoter Score (NPS) of 97, a measure of customer loyalty that far exceeds the industry average.[20] [21]

This high level of customer satisfaction reinforces brand loyalty, as evidenced by Tesla's market-leading retention rate, with 74.7% of Tesla owners purchasing another Tesla vehicle.[22] By prioritizing customer needs and preferences in both sales and service, Tesla has set a new benchmark for automotive companies, highlighting the importance of consumer-centric innovation in the industry.

ADAPT TO SURVIVE

Tesla is rapidly changing the automotive landscape, and traditional dealerships face an urgent need to adapt to remain relevant. With the emergence of direct-to-consumer sales models, dealerships must innovate to meet the new expectations of modern consumers who prioritize convenience and transparency.

If they fail to adjust their practices, dealerships risk being bypassed by both manufacturers and consumers who increasingly favor more streamlined buying processes. The traditional dealership model, characterized by lengthy negotiations and multiple touchpoints, is becoming less appealing to buyers who are accustomed to the ease of online shopping. To stay competitive, dealerships must enhance their customer experience by adopting digital tools, simplifying transactions, and focusing on delivering exceptional value.

The success of Tesla's direct-to-consumer sales model has demonstrated the viability of bypassing traditional dealerships altogether, prompting other automakers to explore similar approaches. This shift toward direct manufacturer-consumer interaction has the potential to significantly alter the role of dealerships. Instead of serving as the primary sales channel, dealerships may evolve into service centers or local representatives that facilitate test drives and vehicle delivery.

Automakers like Tesla are increasingly interested in maintaining control over the customer relationship from start to finish, reducing the dependence on third-party dealerships. Traditional dealerships must redefine their roles by emphasizing service excellence, customer engagement, and personalized experiences to remain vital to the automotive ecosystem.

HYUNDAI AND FORD

Tesla isn't the only automotive company fixated on the direct-to-consumer model. Hyundai and Ford are actively exploring direct sales models that leverage technology to streamline the car-buying process and reduce reliance on traditional dealership interactions too.

Hyundai has begun experimenting with direct sales through platforms like Amazon, allowing consumers to handle much of the purchasing process online. This innovative approach enables customers to explore vehicle options, customize features, and secure financing from the comfort of their homes. By simplifying the purchasing journey, Hyundai provides a more convenient and efficient experience, appealing to tech-savvy buyers who value speed and simplicity. This model also reflects a broader trend toward integrating e-commerce practices into the automotive industry, aligning with consumer preferences for digital transactions.

Ford has begun transitioning toward a direct-to-consumer (DTC) sales model, particularly for its EVs. This move is part of Ford's broader strategy, called "Ford+," which aims to enhance the customer experience and compete with Tesla's successful DTC model. Under this new approach, customers can buy EVs directly from Ford through online platforms, bypassing traditional dealerships for many aspects of the process.

While Ford has not entirely abandoned dealerships, the company is giving customers more options for a streamlined and transparent purchasing experience. For example, Ford's "Model e" division offers transparent, no-haggle pricing and gives customers the flexibility to choose between online or in-store purchasing and home delivery options. However, not all Ford vehicles are sold this way. The DTC approach mainly applies to their EV lineup, and traditional dealerships still handle sales for combustion-engine vehicles and hybrids.

Ford's plan to introduce DTC sales is still evolving, as legal roadblocks exist in several US states due to longstanding dealership franchise laws that prohibit direct vehicle sales to consumers. Despite these challenges, Ford's DTC model aims to improving customer satisfaction through a more seamless, user-friendly sales experience.[23] [24]

Ford's efforts to embrace this model highlight a significant shift in the automotive industry, as manufacturers recognize the need to innovate and adapt to changing consumer expectations. By focusing on direct interaction with customers, Ford aims to build stronger relationships and foster brand loyalty, positioning itself for success in a competitive market.

By leveraging online platforms and direct sales strategies, Hyundai and Ford are setting new standards for convenience and efficiency in the car-buying process. As more automakers explore similar approaches, traditional dealerships must adapt to remain relevant, focusing on enhancing service, building customer trust, and offering unique value propositions that complement these emerging sales models.

THE RISE OF DIRECT SALES

While the shift toward direct sales models presents challenges for traditional dealerships, it also offers significant opportunities for differentiation. As manufacturers and online platforms streamline the car-buying process, dealerships can set themselves apart by focusing on superior customer service and personalized experiences that cannot be matched by direct-to-consumer models. By capitalizing on these strengths, dealerships can position themselves as essential partners in the automotive ecosystem and create lasting value for their customers.

Superior customer service, where the customer's needs come first, is one of the key areas where dealerships can excel. Unlike online-only models, dealerships have the advantage of face-to-face interactions, allowing them to build strong personal relationships with customers. By creating a one-touch experience and training staff to provide transparent pricing and attentive, knowledgeable, and empathetic service, dealerships can enhance customer satisfaction and loyalty. A welcoming and responsive service environment can make the car-buying and ownership experience more enjoyable, encouraging customers to return for future purchases and recommend the dealership to others.

Personalized experiences are another powerful differentiator for dealerships. By understanding each customer's unique needs and preferences, dealerships can tailor their offerings to provide customized solutions. This might include personalized vehicle recommendations and tailored maintenance plans. By going above and beyond, dealerships can deliver experiences that resonate with individual customers, making them feel valued and understood.

While the rise of direct sales models presents challenges, it also opens up opportunities for dealerships to differentiate themselves by offering superior customer service and personalized experiences. By focusing on these strengths, dealerships can thrive in the evolving automotive landscape and continue to play a vital role in connecting consumers with the vehicles they love. Embracing these opportunities for differentiation allows dealerships to build a strong, loyal customer base and maintain their competitive edge in the market.

A FUTURE OF COLLABORATION

The automotive industry is undergoing a profound transformation as the shift toward direct-to-consumer sales models challenges the traditional dealership framework. While these changes present significant challenges, they also offer dealerships a unique opportunity to redefine their roles and deliver unparalleled value to consumers. By embracing change and focusing on delivering exceptional customer service and personalized experiences, dealerships can position themselves as essential partners in the automotive ecosystem.

As the industry continues to evolve, those dealerships that prioritize innovation and customer satisfaction will be best equipped to thrive and maintain their relevance in a rapidly changing market.

Manufacturers like Tesla, Hyundai, and Ford have pioneered new sales approaches, so the pressure for dealerships to innovate is greater than ever. This pressure is *also* a catalyst for growth and improvement. By putting the customer's needs first and focusing on what makes the dealership experience unique, automotive dealers can offer a level of service and personalization that direct-to-consumer models cannot match. The ability to build personal relationships and provide tailored solutions creates a compelling reason for consumers to choose dealerships over direct-to-consumer car companies.

The future of the automotive industry is one of collaboration between manufacturers and dealerships, where each plays to its strengths to deliver a superior customer experience. Manufacturers bring innovation and efficiency, while dealerships offer personalized service and support that enhances the overall ownership journey. By working together, they can ensure that consumers enjoy the best of both worlds: technological advancement paired with human connection and expertise.

This symbiotic relationship promises a bright future for the automotive industry, where both manufacturers and dealerships contribute to a more seamless and satisfying consumer experience.

The shift toward direct-to-consumer models marks a pivotal moment in the automotive industry. For dealerships, this is not a time to resist change but to embrace it as an opportunity to innovate and lead. By focusing on customer-centric strategies and leveraging their unique strengths, dealerships can remain indispensable to consumers and manufacturers alike.

As the automotive landscape continues to evolve, those who adapt will not only survive but flourish, driving the industry forward into a new era of success and customer satisfaction.

CONCLUSION

Toyota #3 was a mess when I first bought into it. Operations were shady, and customer satisfaction was at an all-time low. The store was averaging 60–70 cars per month; on its best month, it sold 80. Its numbers were pitiful.

Today, we sell more than 200 cars a month at that dealership, and our best month?

In October, 2023, we sold 236.

At the store, our Toyota sales efficiency consistently ranks among the highest in the region, reaching levels as high as 290–300%. Every OEM measures efficiency differently, but for Toyota, our performance stands out. We've not only hit these high percentages, but we've maintained them year after year.

A huge part of our success stems from earning the prestigious Toyota President's Award, a highly coveted recognition within the industry. One of the primary metrics for this award is customer retention, which directly reflects the level of satisfaction we're delivering. In fact, since I've been at Toyota #3, we've won the President's Award every single year—a streak that never existed before.

The metrics for winning this award are stringent. It's not just about sales efficiency; consumer satisfaction plays a pivotal role as well. By maintaining a balance between these two factors, we've built a reputation for excellence that's consistently recognized at the highest levels. The results speak for themselves and are a testament to the dedication of our team to deliver top-tier service and satisfaction to our customers.

And our customers are so happy they keep coming back. Our customer retention numbers are through the roof; in 2023, we were #1 in the region for Toyota's Loyalty & Engagement (TLE).

Modern consumers increasingly prioritize convenience, transparency, and ease in their transactions, a shift that is driving significant changes in dealership models. Today's buyers are accustomed to the seamless experiences provided by e-commerce platforms, where products can be researched, purchased, and delivered with just a few clicks. This expectation for simplicity and speed has extended into the automotive industry, where traditional dealership practices often clash with consumer desires.

The lengthy negotiations, complex paperwork, and multiple touchpoints typical of traditional car buying are becoming less appealing to consumers who value streamlined processes. Dealerships are under pressure to innovate and adapt their models to meet these evolving preferences. This includes integrating digital tools that allow customers to complete most of the buying process online, offering transparent pricing and financing options, and providing hassle-free service experiences.

Dealerships must adapt by offering more straightforward, customer-friendly experiences. As consumers increasingly seek the convenience and transparency found in digital purchasing platforms, dealerships are under pressure to transform their operations to meet these expectations. This involves simplifying the car-buying process, from initial research to final purchase, to reduce friction and enhance the overall customer experience.

If they embrace these changes, dealerships can align themselves with consumer expectations and maintain their relevance in an increasingly competitive market.

ESSENTIAL PHILOSOPHIES AND STRATEGIES

The automotive industry has long struggled with a negative reputation, often labeled as sleazy or dishonest, and I absolutely hate that perception because I love this industry. Yes, there have been dishonorable practices that have contributed to this image, but that doesn't mean dealerships need to operate this way to be successful. Too many businesses focus on the aftermath of the sale, which fosters bad habits and negative customer experiences.

This book aims to refocus the conversation, showing how to secure the sale from the beginning by genuinely putting the customer first. I believe in running a dealership with integrity, transparency, and trust. The industry doesn't have to live under the cloud of distrust. It's entirely possible to run a successful dealership in a positive, transparent environment where customers are treated fairly and respectfully.

It would be devastating to see an industry that has provided for my family since I was 17 continue to be attacked and maligned, especially when I know we can operate in a way that people respect and appreciate. Why can't we, as dealerships, be seen as helpful? Why can't we elevate this industry to a point where people are proud to work in it and customers are genuinely happy with their purchases?

This industry has given me so much, and I'm committed to reshaping it into something that others can be proud of too.

If one of my children was in the industry and was going to meet the successful parents of someone they were dating, I would want their reaction to my child's profession in the automotive industry to be positive.

The purpose of this book is to equip dealership owners and managers with the essential philosophies and strategies to modernize their operations and enhance customer experience in an ever-changing automotive industry. As consumer preferences continue to evolve rapidly, the traditional dealership model faces increasing pressure to adapt and innovate.

Today's consumers demand convenience, transparency, and efficiency in their interactions with dealerships, challenging the industry to rethink and reshape its approach. This book serves as a comprehensive guide for dealership leaders who recognize the need for transformation and are committed to leading their organizations into a new era of customer engagement and operational excellence.

At the heart of this transformation is a commitment to customer satisfaction. The book emphasizes the importance of creating a customer-centric environment and a one-touch experience that prioritize the needs and preferences of consumers. This involves fostering a culture of empathy and service excellence, where every interaction is an opportunity to build trust and foster loyalty. By understanding and anticipating customer needs, dealerships can tailor their offerings to provide personalized experiences that resonate with buyers and encourage repeat business.

To truly thrive, dealerships must also focus on streamlining their processes to eliminate inefficiencies and reduce friction in the customer journey. This involves reevaluating every aspect of the dealership's operations, from sales and service to finance and customer support. By adopting lean principles and optimizing workflows, dealerships can enhance their productivity and responsiveness, ensuring that they meet the needs of customers promptly and effectively.

And through a series of actionable insights and real-world examples, dealership leaders can learn how to implement these strategies effectively.

It's time for dealership owners and managers like you to embrace change and seize the opportunity to transform their operations. By adopting the philosophies and strategies outlined in these pages, you can lead your dealership into a new era of excellence, where customer satisfaction and operational efficiency go hand in hand. The journey toward modernization is not without its challenges, but with the right tools and mindset, you can navigate this landscape successfully and emerge as a leader in the automotive industry.

HOW TO IMPLEMENT THESE PHILOSOPHIES

My philosophies can be implemented by anyone. If you adhere to the practices laid out in this book, you can implement these philosophies and turn around your dealership.

For those of you who want an edge, I offer consultancy services to assist dealerships in effectively implementing these transformative changes. The transition from traditional dealership models to modern, customer-focused operations can be complex, requiring a nuanced understanding of both the industry and individual dealership dynamics.

Together with an amazing team, I have turned around dealership after dealership because I have years of industry experience and a deep understanding of the challenges facing modern dealerships. I have the expertise needed to seamlessly guide the transition.

I recognize that the specific needs and circumstances of each dealership are different—there is no one-size-fits-all solution. I work closely with clients to understand their unique challenges and objectives, developing tailored strategies that align with their goals. This personalized approach ensures that the solutions implemented are not only effective but also sustainable, providing long-term value for the dealership and its customers.

I assist dealerships in navigating the complexities of transformation, from integrating digital tools and optimizing processes to enhancing customer experiences and building a culture of innovation. My expert guidance helps dealership leaders implement my philosophies to overcome common obstacles, avoid pitfalls, and capitalize on opportunities for growth and improvement. Whether it's training staff on new technologies, redesigning workflows for greater efficiency, or developing strategies for customer engagement, I provide the resources and insights needed to drive successful outcomes.

I also focus on fostering a culture of continuous improvement within dealerships. I encourage leaders and teams to embrace change as an ongoing process, equipping them with the skills and mindset needed to adapt to evolving market conditions and consumer expectations. This ensures that dealerships remain competitive in the dynamic automotive landscape, positioning them for success in a future that demands agility and innovation.

Together, we can transform challenges into opportunities, building a stronger, more resilient dealership that delivers exceptional value to customers and achieves long-term success.

PROACTIVELY MODERNIZE YOUR DEALERSHIP

The call to action for you is clear: embrace these new practices and take proactive steps to modernize your dealership.

As the automotive industry continues to evolve at an unprecedented pace as automakers like Tesla, Hyundai, and Ford embrace the direct-to-consumer model, it is imperative for dealership owners and managers like you to not only keep up with these changes but to actively lead the way in transforming the customer experience. This book is a guide to critically assessing your current operations, identifying areas of improvement and adopting innovative strategies that prioritize customer needs and enhance operational efficiency. By doing so, you position your dealerships to not only survive but thrive in a competitive market.

Critically assessing your operations involves a thorough evaluation of existing processes, identifying pain points and inefficiencies that may hinder customer satisfaction and business growth. This book provides you with the tools to conduct this evaluation, offering insights into industry best practices and emerging trends that can be leveraged to your advantage. From integrating cutting-edge technology to fostering a customer-centric culture, the 19 philosophies outlined in this book are designed to help you reimagine every aspect of your dealership's operations.

Adopting these new philosophies requires a commitment to change and a willingness to challenge the status quo. It involves empowering your team with the knowledge and skills they need to deliver exceptional service and embracing technological advancements that streamline processes and enhance the customer experience. By prioritizing customer needs, you not only build trust and loyalty but also create a sustainable competitive edge that sets your dealership apart.

Should you require additional support or guidance on this transformative journey, do not hesitate to reach out for further assistance. I am dedicated to helping you implement these changes effectively and navigating any challenges that may arise along the way. Together, we can redefine what it means to be a successful dealership in today's market, building a sustainable future that benefits both your business and your customers.

Embrace the opportunity to innovate, and join the movement toward a more efficient, customer-focused automotive industry.

ACKNOWLEDGMENTS

First off, to my family: thank you for putting up with me during this whole process. I know I've spent even less time at home, and the time had to come from somewhere. I couldn't exactly sell fewer cars, so I know you all got less of me, and I appreciate your patience and understanding more than I can say.

Next, a huge shoutout to my editor, Lisa Caskey. This has been a massive project, and I couldn't have done it without you. Your insight and dedication have been a game changer, and I'm incredibly grateful for your help every step of the way.

And of course, a big thank you to Scribe. Your team played a huge role in getting this book out into the world, and I appreciate all the hard work that went into making it happen.

ABOUT THE AUTHOR

JASON QUENNEVILLE is a seasoned automotive executive, dealership operator, and racing enthusiast with over two decades of experience transforming underperforming dealerships into high-performing, customer-centric businesses. Since starting his career in the automotive industry in 1998, Jason has worked his way up from washing cars at a Chevrolet dealership to co-owning and operating multiple successful Toyota and Mazda dealerships in New Hampshire.

His passion for the industry is deeply rooted in his belief that customer experience is the key to dealership success. Through his 19 customer-centric philosophies, he has led dealerships from the brink of closure to ranking among the top in their regions, consistently achieving industry-leading sales efficiency. His innovative approach—focusing on transparency, long-term relationships, and streamlined operations—has reshaped how car dealerships operate, mirroring the convenience and efficiency of online shopping.

Beyond the automotive world, Jason is an avid dirt modified race car driver, drawing parallels between the precision and strategy of racing and the agility required to run a successful dealership. His commitment to excellence and relentless drive have not only built thriving businesses but also created positive, sustainable workplace cultures for his teams.

Jason's insights and strategies are captured in his book *Green Green Green: 19 Customer-Centric Philosophies to Drive Your Dealership's Growth*, where he shares the lessons, challenges, and transformative practices that have defined his career. His mission is to help dealership owners, general managers, and industry leaders embrace change, exceed customer expectations, and future-proof their businesses.

NOTES

1 Felton, Ryan, "Discounts on the Dealership Lot Lift Car Sales," *The Wall Street Journal*, December 29, 2024, https://www.wsj.com/business/autos/auto-industry-sales-tariff-outlook-25bfc816.

2 Eckert, Nora, "Consumers Boosted 2024 U.S. New-Car Sales to Five-Year High," Reuters, January 3, 2025. https://www.reuters.com/business/autos-transportation/consumers-boosted-2024-us-new-car-sales-five-year-high-2025-01-03.

3 James, Talia and Mitch Paul, "Uncharted Territory: Edmunds Forecasts 16.2 Million New Vehicle Sales in 2025 Amid Policy Uncertainty, Ongoing Affordability Challenges," Edmunds, December 17, 2024, https://www.edmunds.com/industry/press/uncharted-territory-edmunds-forecasts-16-2-million-new-vehicle-sales-in-2025-amid-policy-uncertainty-ongoing-affordability-challenges.html.

4 Smoke, Jonathan, "Forecast: 2024—Cox Automotive Inc.," January 8, 2024, https://www.coxautoinc.com/market-insights/forecast-2024/.

5 Cyrus Moulton, "Why Attention Spans Seem to Be Shrinking and What We Can Do About It," Medical Xpress, January 24, 2024, https://medicalxpress.com/news/2024-01-attention-spans.html.

6 Hancock, Ben, "Revolutionizing Retail: Emerging Technologies Reshaping Shopping Experiences," Retail Technology Review, January 30, 2024, https://www.retailtechnologyreview.com/articles/2024/01/30/revolutionizing-retail-emerging-technologies-reshaping-shopping-experiences/.

7 SuperOffice, "Customer Journey: How to Drive Profitable Business Growth," SuperOffice Blog, accessed March 26, 2025, https://www.superoffice.com/blog/customer-journey/.

8 PricewaterhouseCoopers, "Experience Is Everything: Here's How to Get It Right," PwC, accessed February 14, 2025, https://www.pwc.com/us/en/services/consulting/library/consumer-intelligence-series/future-of-customer-experience.html.

9 Evans, Michelle, "Using Retail Tech Innovation to Enhance the Customer Experience," National Retail Federation, June 2021, https://www.anuarioseguros.lat/admin/storage/files/Experiencia_del_cliente.pdf?utm_source=chatgpt.com.

10 Carey, Ruthie, "Why Frictionless Customer Experience Matters in Business?" Five9, November 16, 2023, https://www.five9.com/blog/why-frictionless-customer-experience-matters-business.

11   Broom, Douglas, "Happy Employees Are More Productive, Research Shows," November 13, 2019, https://www.weforum.org/agenda/2019/11/happy-employees-more-productive.

12   Hall, Aaron, "The Power of Employee Benefits: Attracting, Retaining, and Engaging Top Talent," Attorney Aaron Hall, October 29, 2023, https://aaronhall.com/the-power-of-employee-benefits-attracting-retaining-and-engaging-top-talent.

13   TriNet, "Impact of Employee Benefits on Recruitment and Retention," TriNet, May 31, 2024, https://www.trinet.com/insights/impact-of-employee-benefits-on-recruitment-and-retention.

14   Enrich, "How to Create an Impressive Benefits Package to Attract and Retain High-Quality Employees," Enrich, August 28, 2023, https://www.trinet.com/insights/impact-of-employee-benefits-on-recruitment-and-retention.

15   Ellering, Nathan, "2023 Texting and SMS Marketing Statistics," SimpleTexting, May 31, 2023, https://simpletexting.com/blog/2023-texting-and-sms-marketing-statistics.

16   Magaline, Vince, "SMS Marketing Statistics," Customers.ai, February 26, 2024, https://customers.ai/blog/sms-marketing-statistics.

17   Calldrip, "Speed to Lead: Your Complete Guide to Lead Response Time," Calldrip, accessed February 14, 2025, https://www.calldrip.com/speed-to-lead.

18   Cooperata, "Are You Responding to Your Customers Too Quickly?," Cooperata, accessed February 14, 2025, https://cooperata.com/are-you-responding-to-your-customers-too-quickly.

19   Molenaar, Koba, "Tesla Stats: Production Stats, Revenue & More [2023]," Influencer Marketing Hub, September 1, 2023, https://influencermarketinghub.com/tesla-stats/.

20   Zahid, Umar, "Driving Brand Loyalty: Lessons From Tesla's Unmatched Customer Experience," Eclipse AI, May 15, 2024, https://eclipse-ai.com/driving-brand-loyalty-lessons-from-teslas-unmatched-customer-experience/.

21   Tessitore, Sabrina, "Tesla's NPS Score: What's Driving Tesla's Customer Loyalty?," NPS Benchmarks, March 13, 2023, https://customergauge.com/benchmarks/blog/tesla-nps-score.

22   Tessitore, Sabrina, "Tesla's NPS Score: What's Driving Tesla's Customer Loyalty?," NPS Benchmarks, March 13, 2023, https://customergauge.com/benchmarks/blog/tesla-nps-score.

23   EnergyTrend, "Ford to Adopt Tesla's NACS Standard for EV Charging, Paving the Way for Other Automakers to Follow," EnergyTrend, June 12, 2023, https://www.energytrend.com/news/20230612-32290.html.

24   Fischer, Justin, "Ford Model E: Ford Will Run Their EV Business Separately, Opening a Path for Direct-to-Consumer Sales," CarEdge, March 23, 2023, https://caredge.com/guides/ford-model-e.